MAX AXIOM
AND THE SOCIETY OF SUPER SCIENTISTS

JOURNEY TO THE
FUTURE OF TRANSPORTATION

BY **AILYNN COLLINS**

ILLUSTRATED BY **DANIEL PEDROSA**

CAPSTONE PRESS
a capstone imprint

Published by Capstone Press, an imprint of Capstone
1710 Roe Crest Drive
North Mankato, Minnesota 56003
capstonepub.com

Library of Congress Cataloging-in-Publication Data
is available on the Library of Congress website.
ISBN: 9781669017295 (hardcover)
ISBN: 9781669017240 (paperback)
ISBN: 9781669017257 (ebook PDF)

Summary: Today most people travel in vehicles powered by fossil fuels.
But what will transportation look like in the future? Will people ride in
cars that drive themselves? Will flying cars from sci-fi films become a
reality? How will advancements in transportation help reduce climate
change? Take a trip with Max Axiom and the Society of Super Scientists to
discover new ways people may travel from place to place in the future.

Editorial Credits
Editor: Aaron Sautter; Designer: Elyse White;
Media Researcher: Rebekah Hubstenberger;
Production Specialist: Whitney Schaefer

All internet sites appearing in back matter were available and accurate
when this book was sent to press.

TABLE OF CONTENTS

THE SOCIETY OF SUPER SCIENTISTS

MAX AXIOM

After years of study, Max Axiom, the world's first Super Scientist, knew the mysteries of the universe were too vast for one person alone to uncover. So Max created the Society of Super Scientists! Using their superpowers and super-smarts, this talented group investigates today's most urgent scientific and environmental issues and learns about actions everyone can take to solve them.

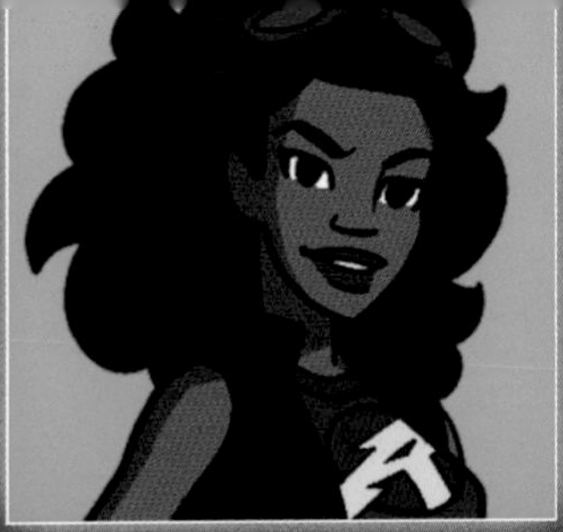

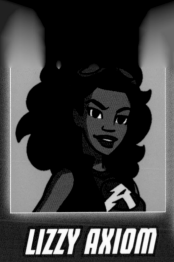

LIZZY AXIOM

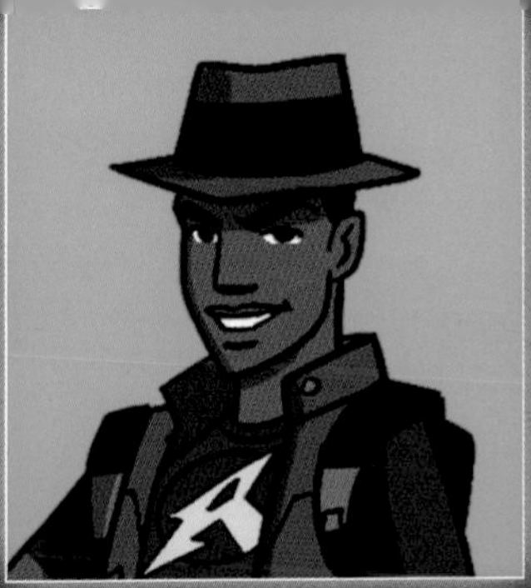

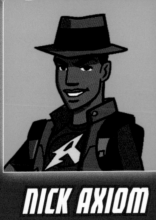

NICK AXIOM

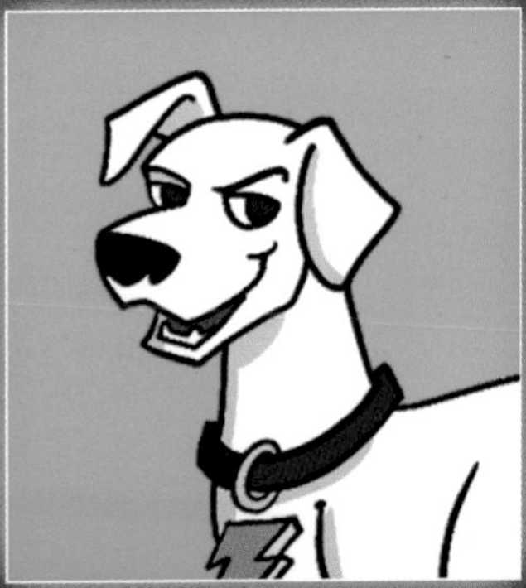

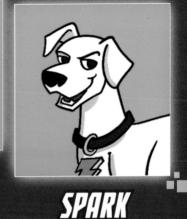

SPARK

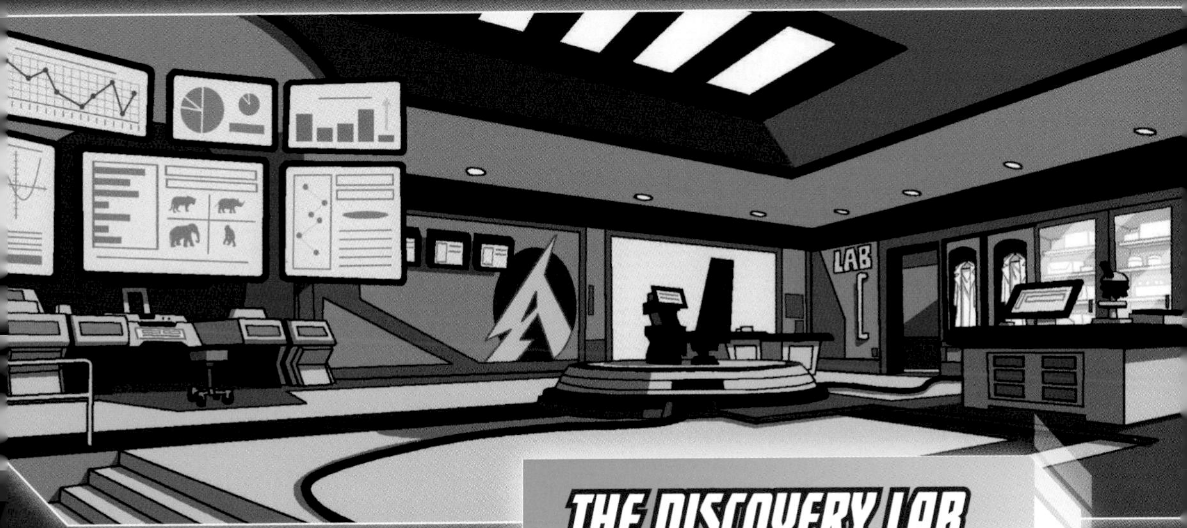
LAB

THE DISCOVERY LAB

Home of the Society of Super Scientists, this state-of-the-art lab houses advanced tools for cutting-edge research and radical scientific innovation. More importantly, it is a space for Super Scientists to collaborate and share knowledge as they work together to tackle any challenge.

SECTION 1: ARE ELECTRIC CARS THE FUTURE?

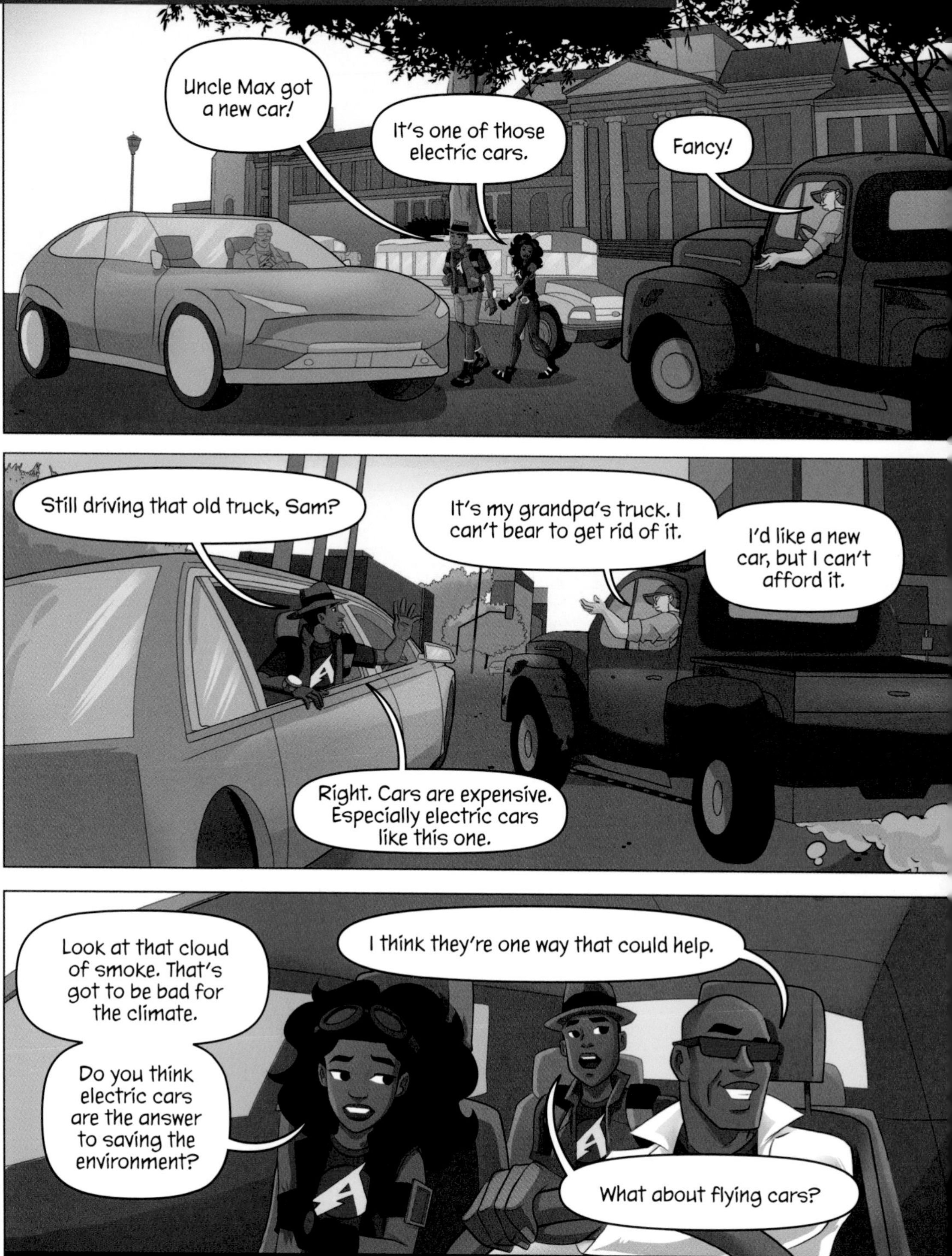
Uncle Max got a new car!
It's one of those electric cars.
Fancy!
Still driving that old truck, Sam?
It's my grandpa's truck. I can't bear to get rid of it.
I'd like a new car, but I can't afford it.
Right. Cars are expensive. Especially electric cars like this one.
Look at that cloud of smoke. That's got to be bad for the climate.
Do you think electric cars are the answer to saving the environment?
I think they're one way that could help.
What about flying cars?

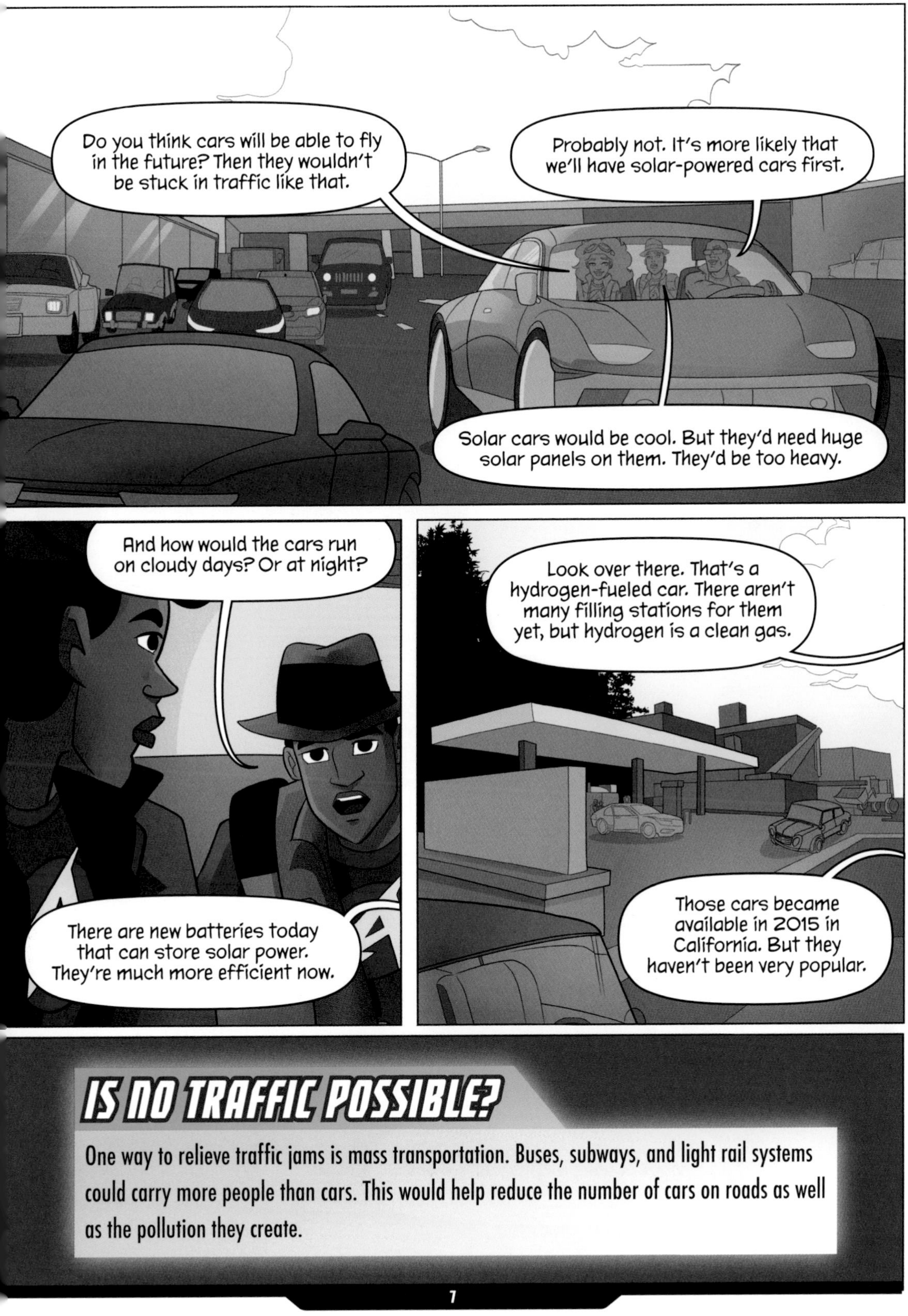
Do you think cars will be able to fly in the future? Then they wouldn't be stuck in traffic like that.
Probably not. It's more likely that we'll have solar-powered cars first.
Solar cars would be cool. But they'd need huge solar panels on them. They'd be too heavy.
And how would the cars run on cloudy days? Or at night?
There are new batteries today that can store solar power. They're much more efficient now.
Look over there. That's a hydrogen-fueled car. There aren't many filling stations for them yet, but hydrogen is a clean gas.
Those cars became available in 2015 in California. But they haven't been very popular.

IS NO TRAFFIC POSSIBLE?

One way to relieve traffic jams is mass transportation. Buses, subways, and light rail systems could carry more people than cars. This would help reduce the number of cars on roads as well as the pollution they create.

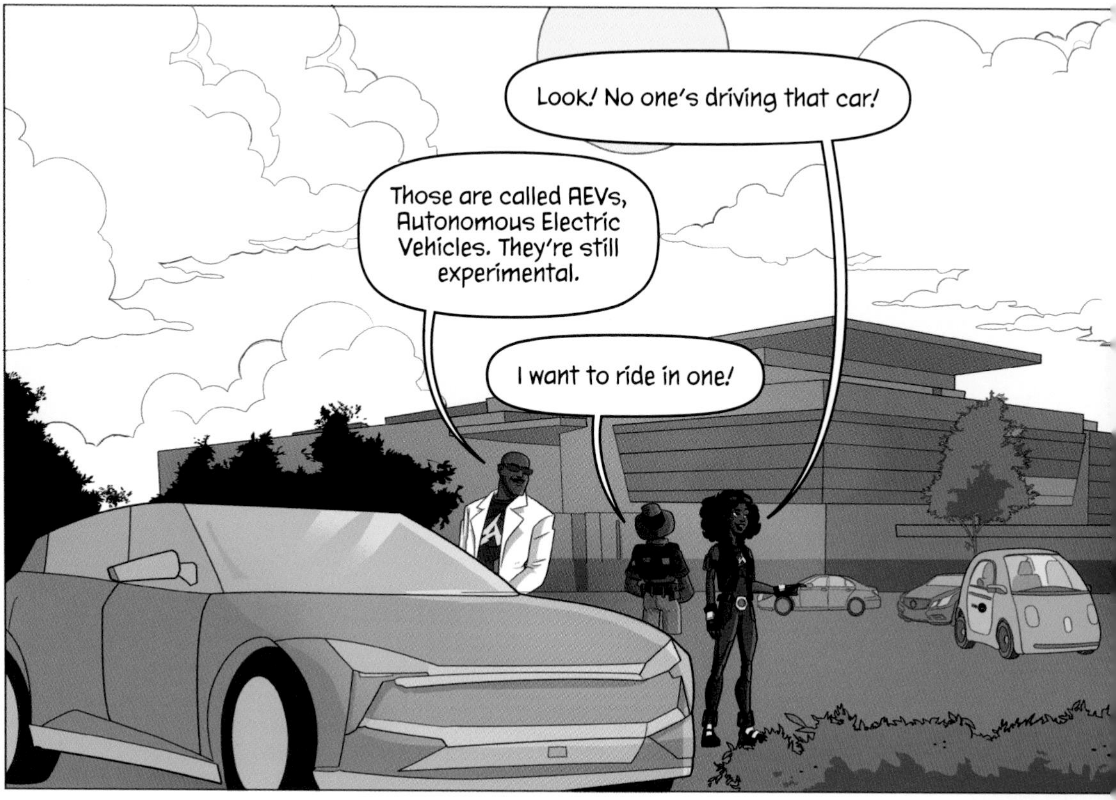
Look! No one's driving that car!
Those are called AEVs, Autonomous Electric Vehicles. They're still experimental.
I want to ride in one!

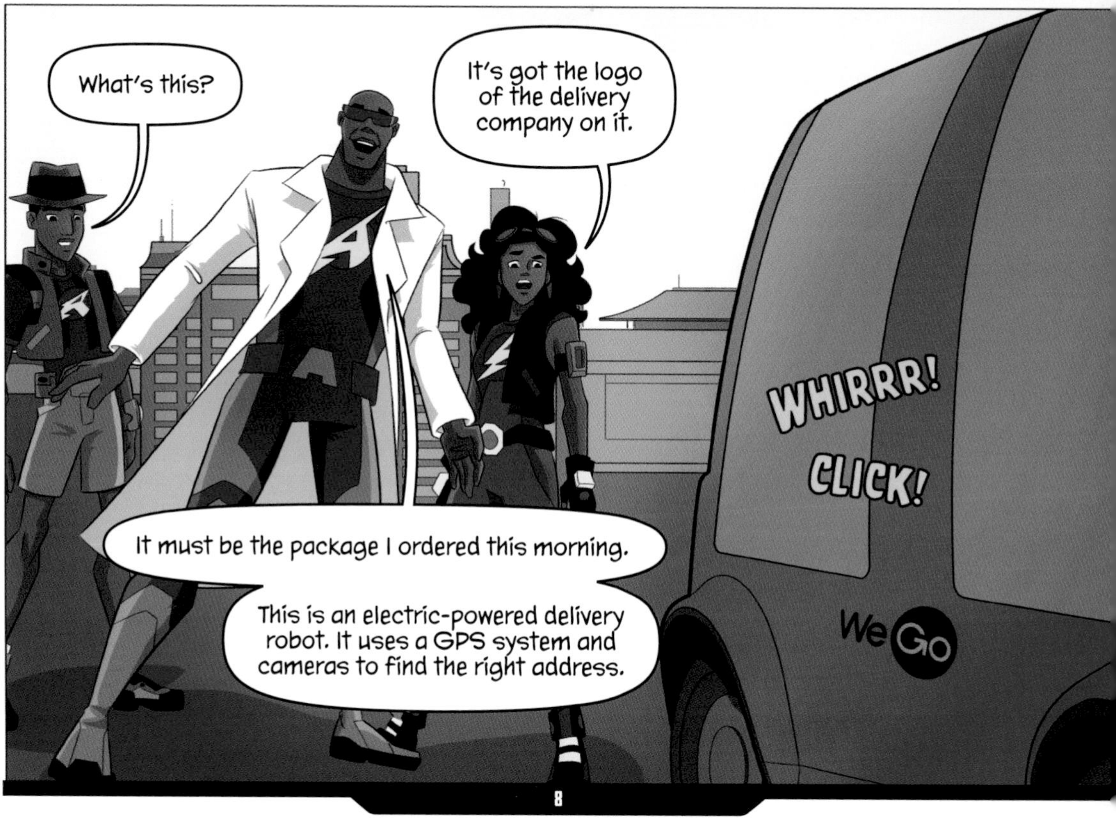
What's this?
It's got the logo of the delivery company on it.
WHIRRR!
CLICK!
It must be the package I ordered this morning.
This is an electric-powered delivery robot. It uses a GPS system and cameras to find the right address.
WeGo

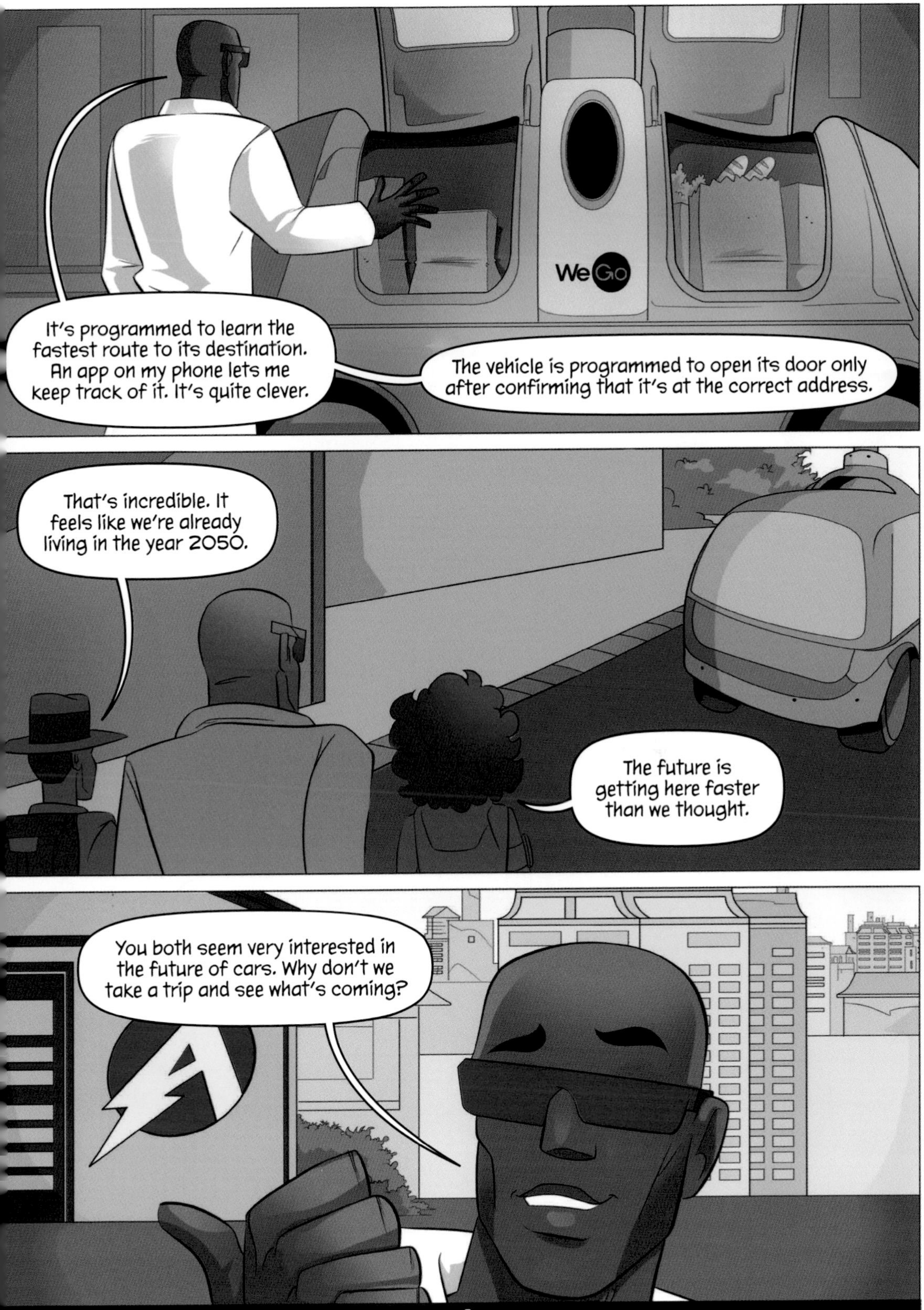
It's programmed to learn the fastest route to its destination. An app on my phone lets me keep track of it. It's quite clever.
The vehicle is programmed to open its door only after confirming that it's at the correct address.
WeGo
That's incredible. It feels like we're already living in the year 2050.
The future is getting here faster than we thought.
You both seem very interested in the future of cars. Why don't we take a trip and see what's coming?

SECTION 2: *OFF TO THE FUTURE*

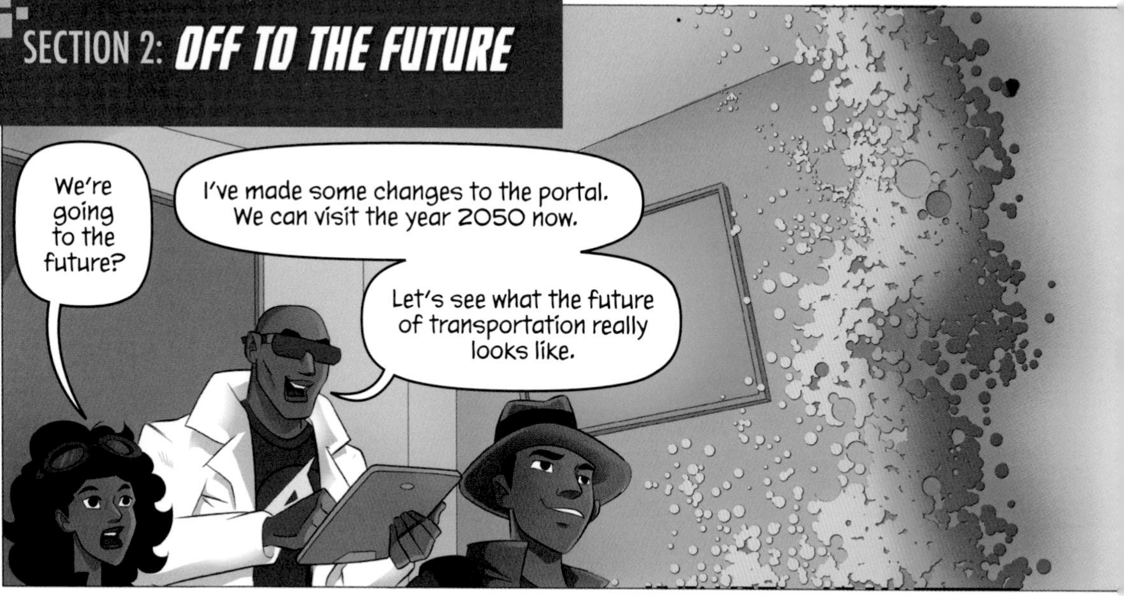
We're going to the future?
I've made some changes to the portal. We can visit the year 2050 now.
Let's see what the future of transportation really looks like.

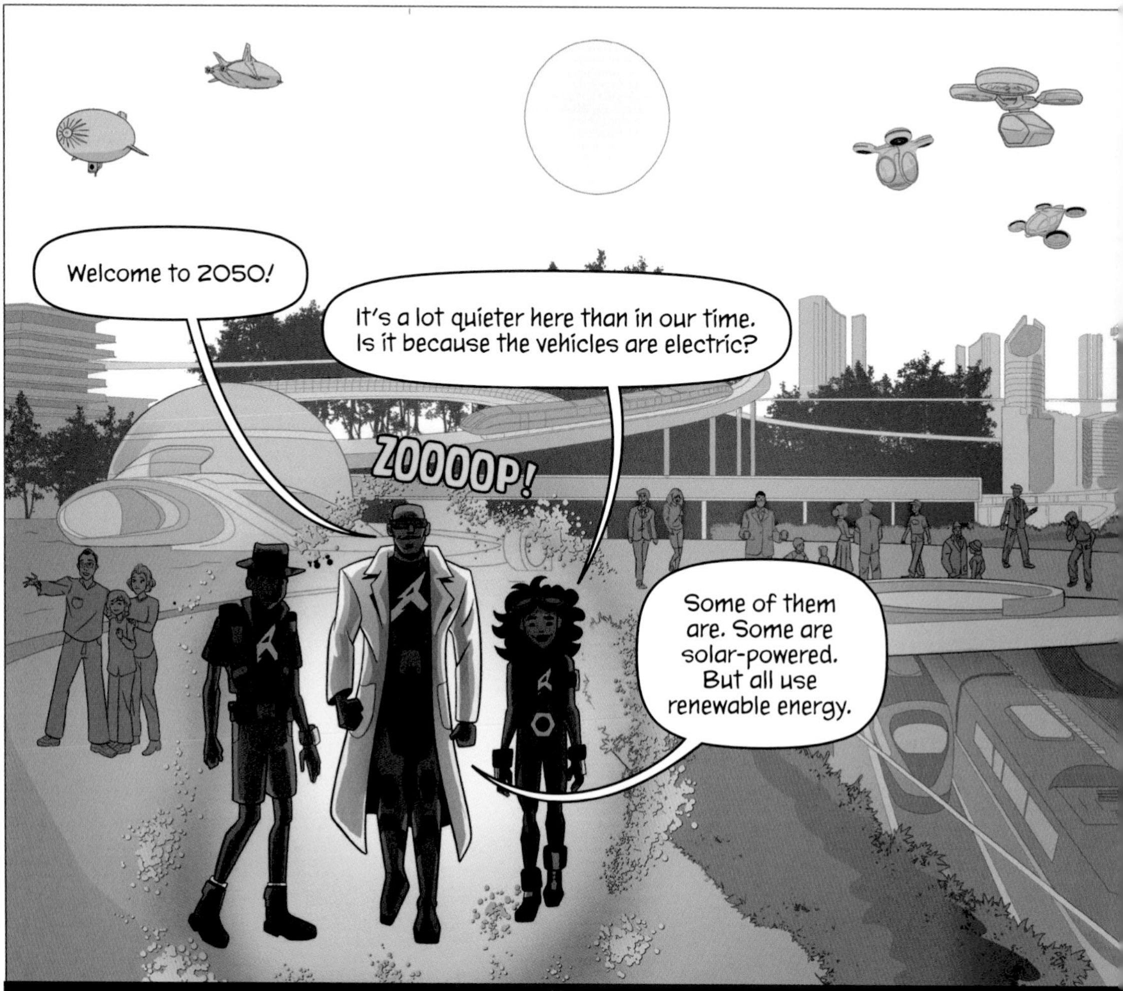
Welcome to 2050!
ZOOOOP!
It's a lot quieter here than in our time. Is it because the vehicles are electric?
Some of them are. Some are solar-powered. But all use renewable energy.

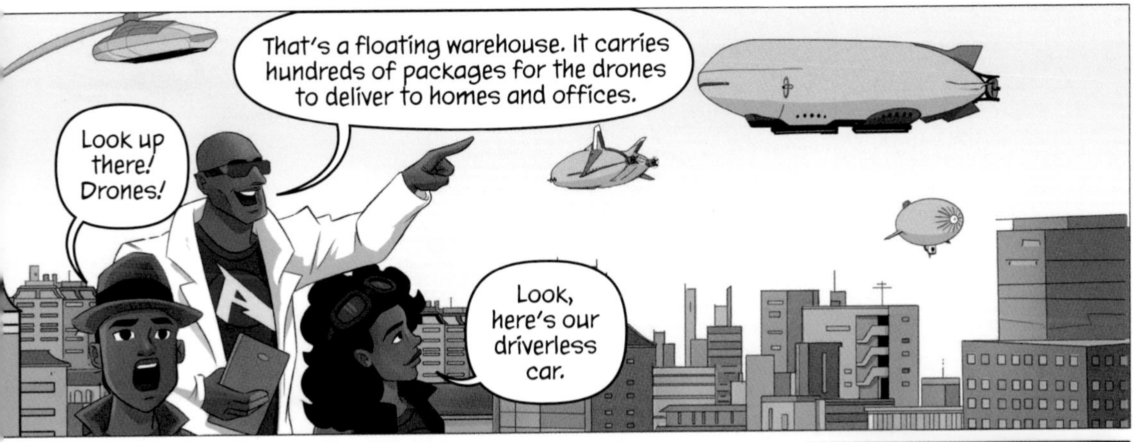
Look up there! Drones!
That's a floating warehouse. It carries hundreds of packages for the drones to deliver to homes and offices.
Look, here's our driverless car.

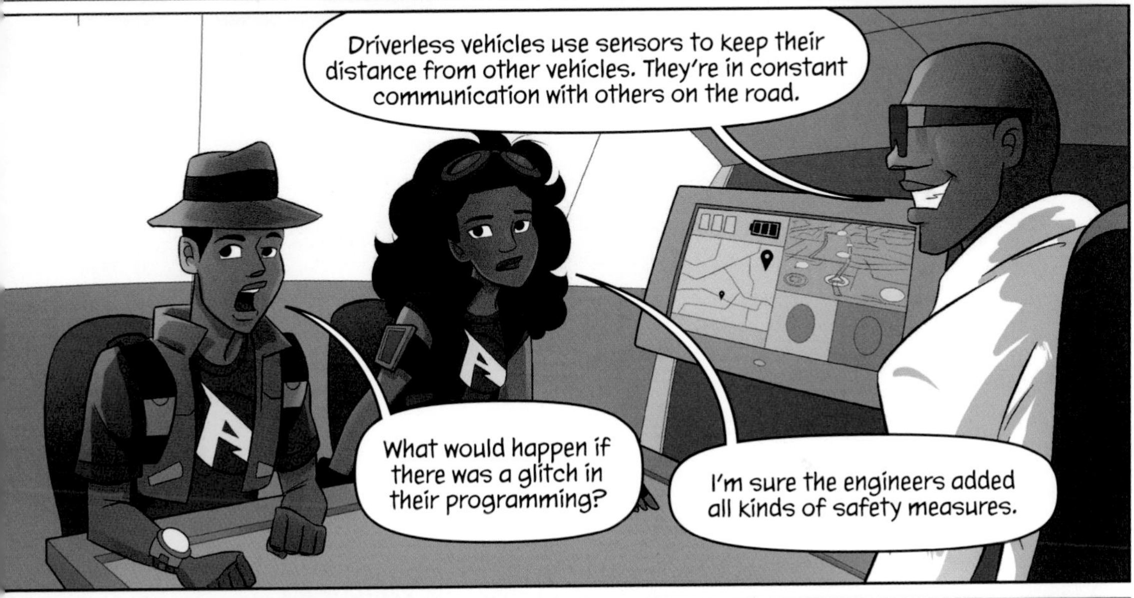
Driverless vehicles use sensors to keep their distance from other vehicles. They're in constant communication with others on the road.
What would happen if there was a glitch in their programming?
I'm sure the engineers added all kinds of safety measures.

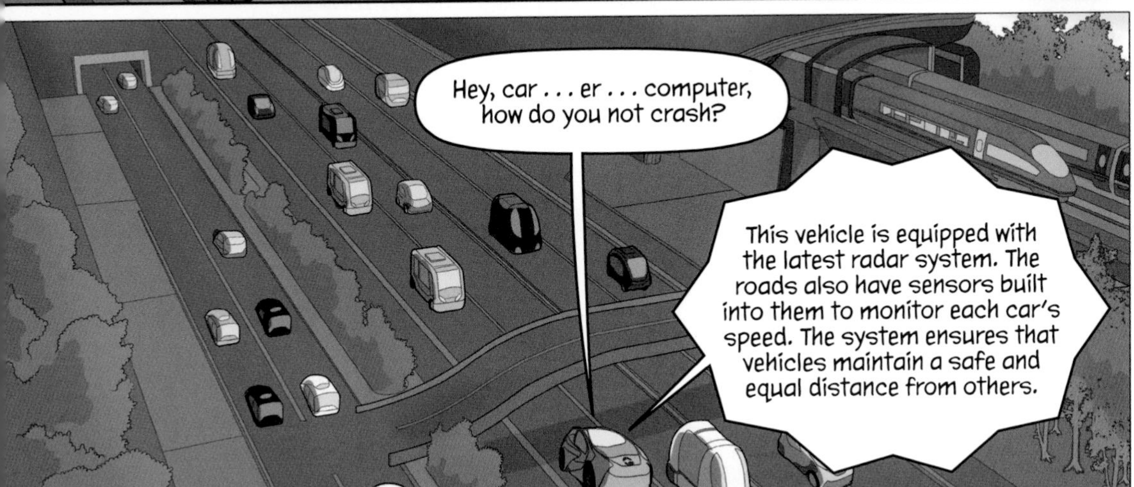
Hey, car . . . er . . . computer, how do you not crash?
This vehicle is equipped with the latest radar system. The roads also have sensors built into them to monitor each car's speed. The system ensures that vehicles maintain a safe and equal distance from others.

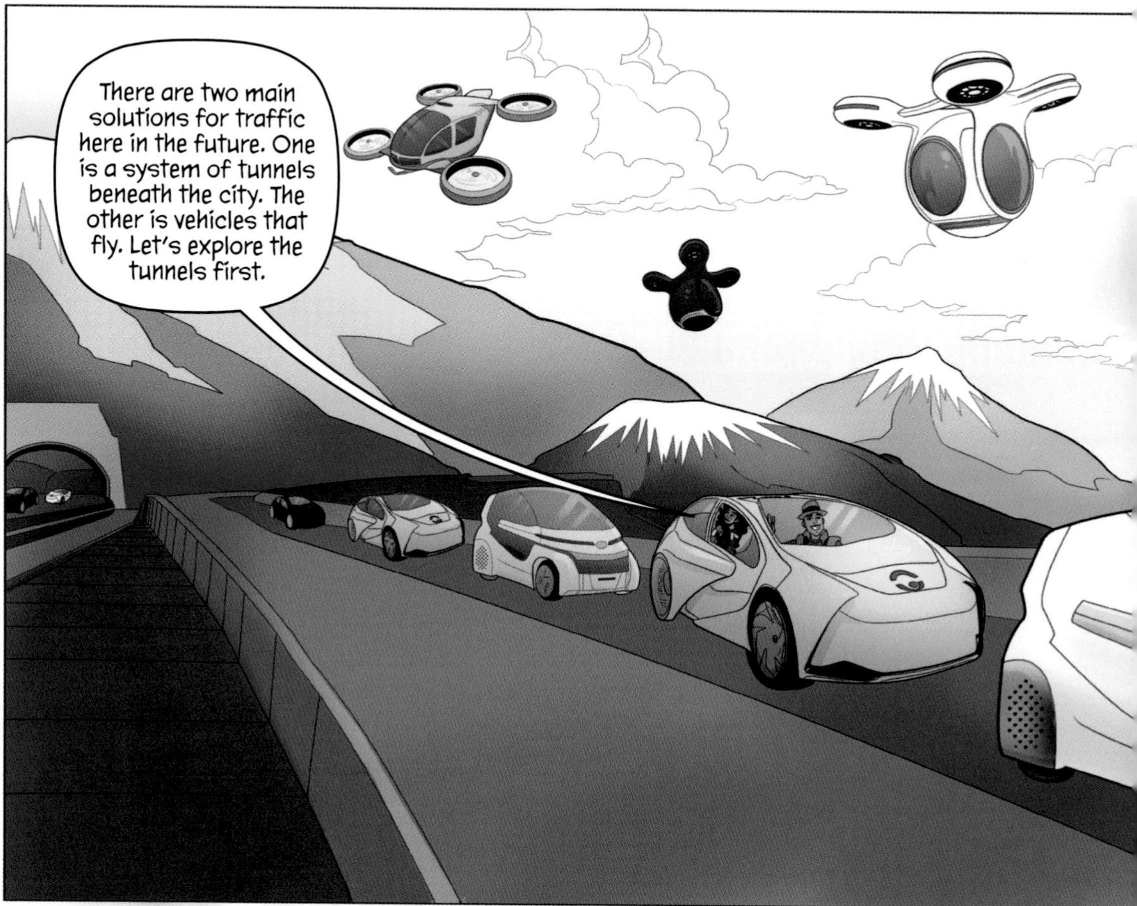
There are two main solutions for traffic here in the future. One is a system of tunnels beneath the city. The other is vehicles that fly. Let's explore the tunnels first.

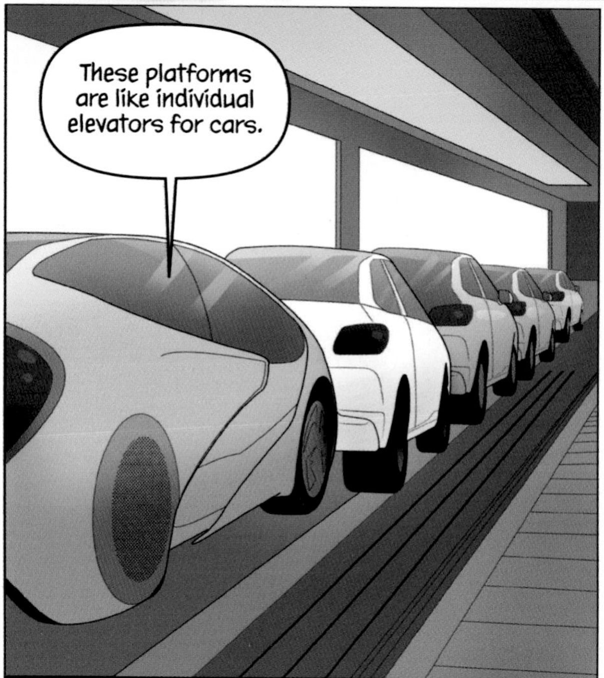
These platforms are like individual elevators for cars.

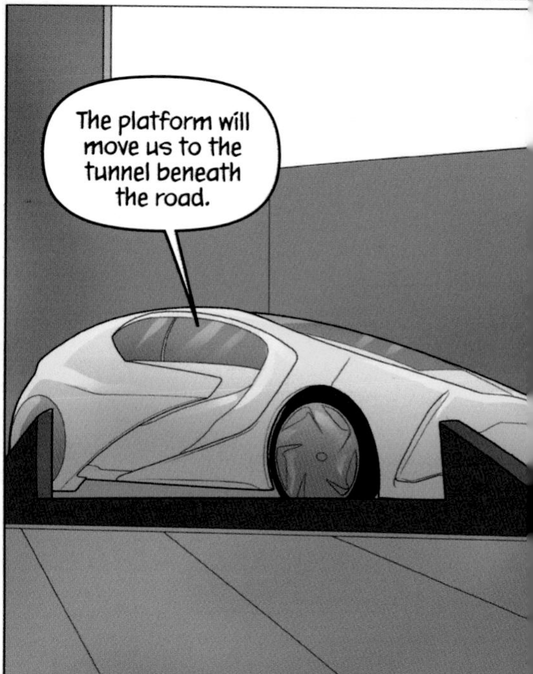
The platform will move us to the tunnel beneath the road.

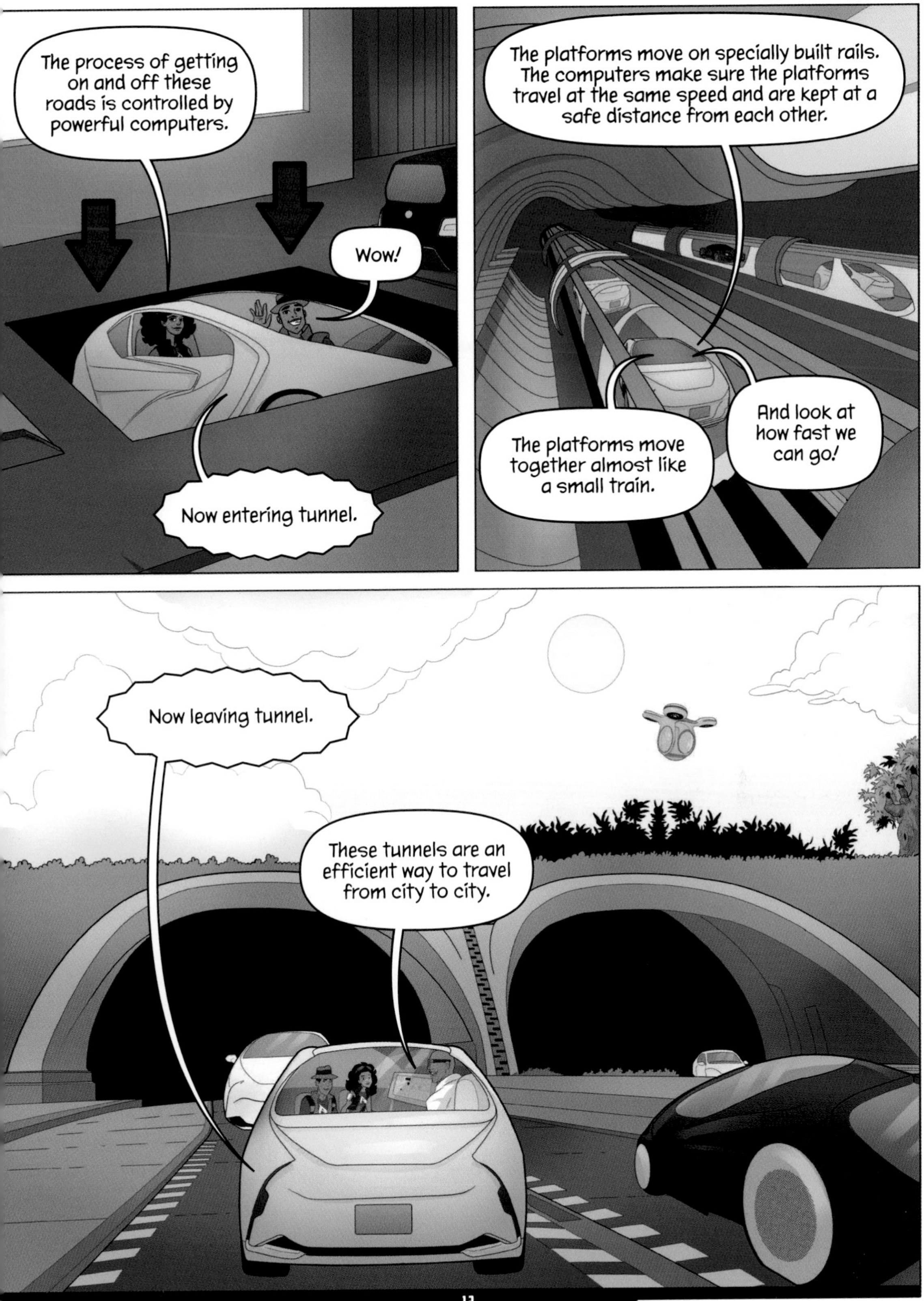
The process of getting on and off these roads is controlled by powerful computers.
Wow!
Now entering tunnel.
The platforms move on specially built rails. The computers make sure the platforms travel at the same speed and are kept at a safe distance from each other.
The platforms move together almost like a small train.
And look at how fast we can go!
Now leaving tunnel.
These tunnels are an efficient way to travel from city to city.

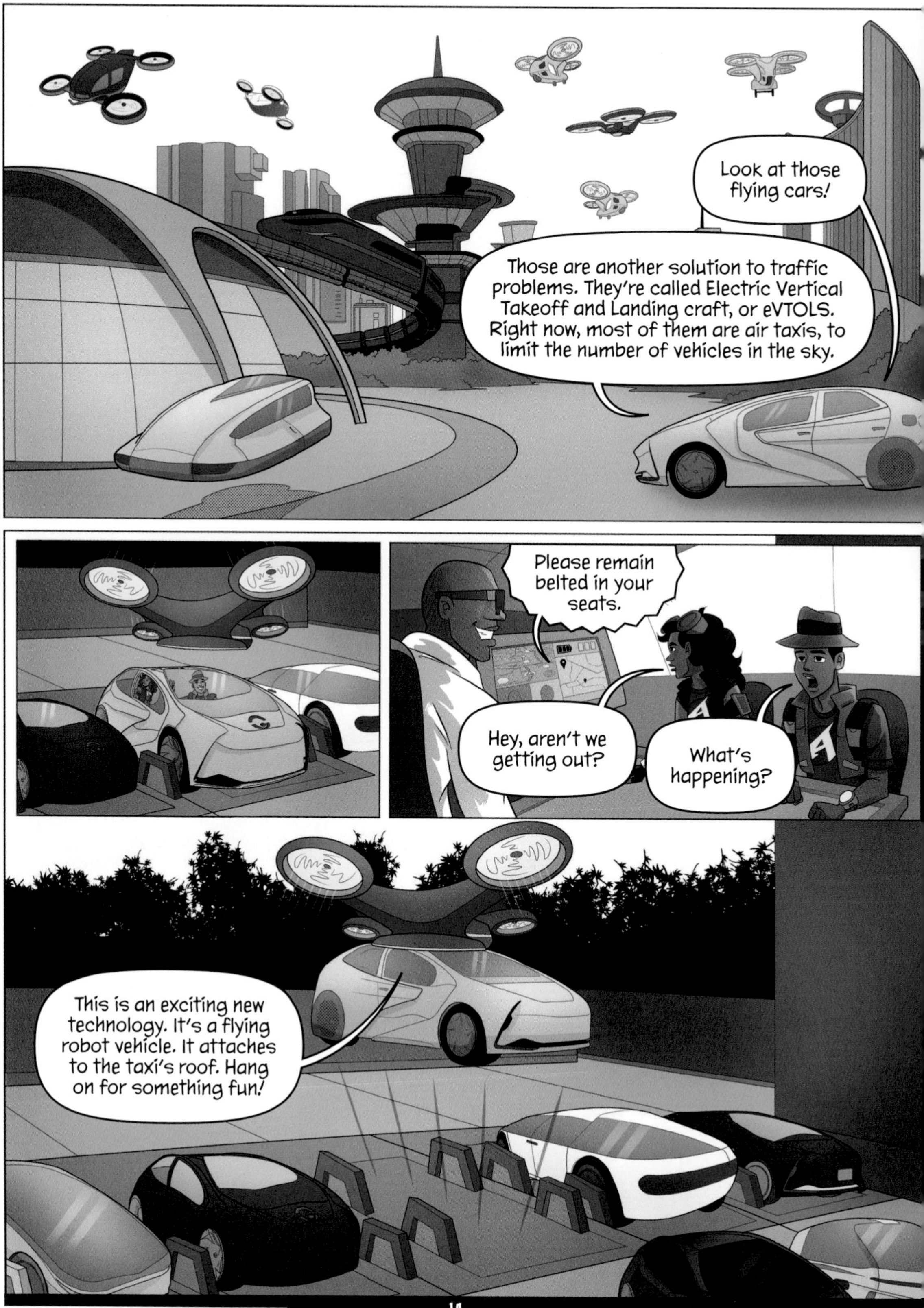
Look at those flying cars!
Those are another solution to traffic problems. They're called Electric Vertical Takeoff and Landing craft, or eVTOLS. Right now, most of them are air taxis, to limit the number of vehicles in the sky.
Please remain belted in your seats.
Hey, aren't we getting out?
What's happening?
This is an exciting new technology. It's a flying robot vehicle. It attaches to the taxi's roof. Hang on for something fun!

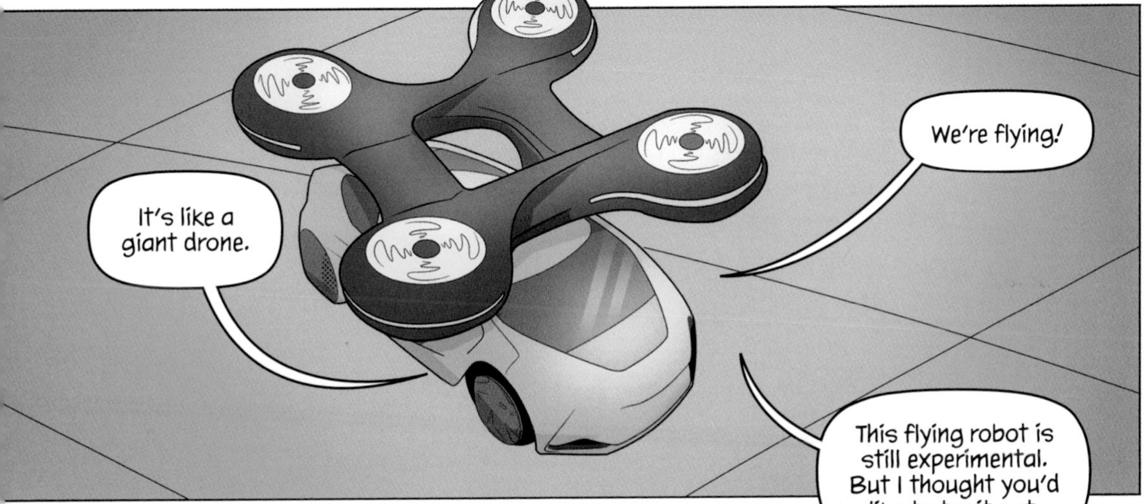
We're flying!
It's like a giant drone.
This flying robot is still experimental. But I thought you'd like to try it out.

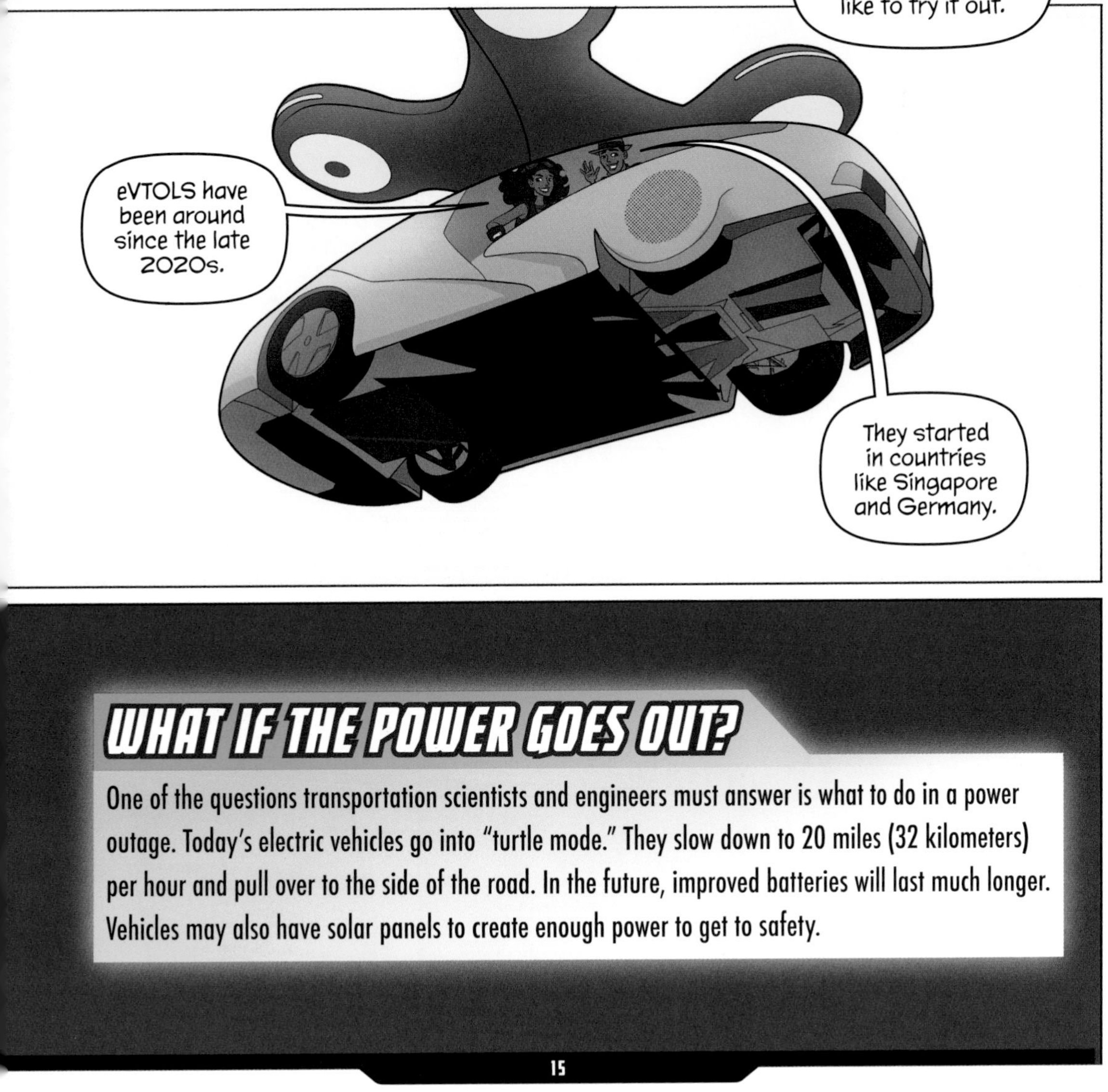
eVTOLS have been around since the late 2020s.
They started in countries like Singapore and Germany.

WHAT IF THE POWER GOES OUT?

One of the questions transportation scientists and engineers must answer is what to do in a power outage. Today's electric vehicles go into "turtle mode." They slow down to 20 miles (32 kilometers) per hour and pull over to the side of the road. In the future, improved batteries will last much longer. Vehicles may also have solar panels to create enough power to get to safety.

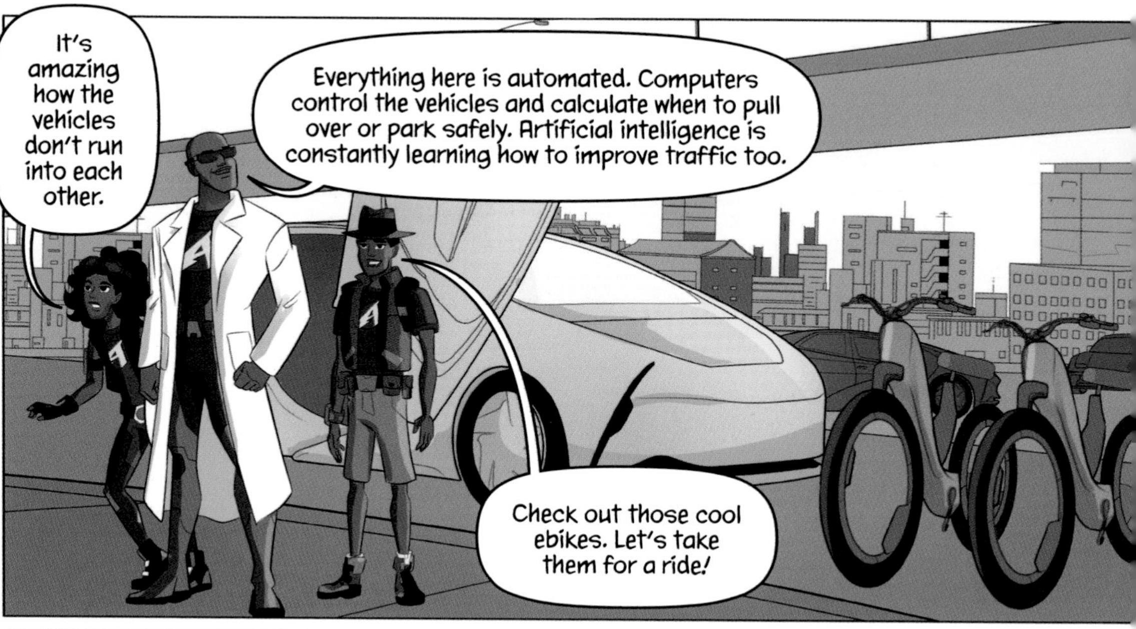
It's amazing how the vehicles don't run into each other.
Everything here is automated. Computers control the vehicles and calculate when to pull over or park safely. Artificial intelligence is constantly learning how to improve traffic too.
Check out those cool ebikes. Let's take them for a ride!

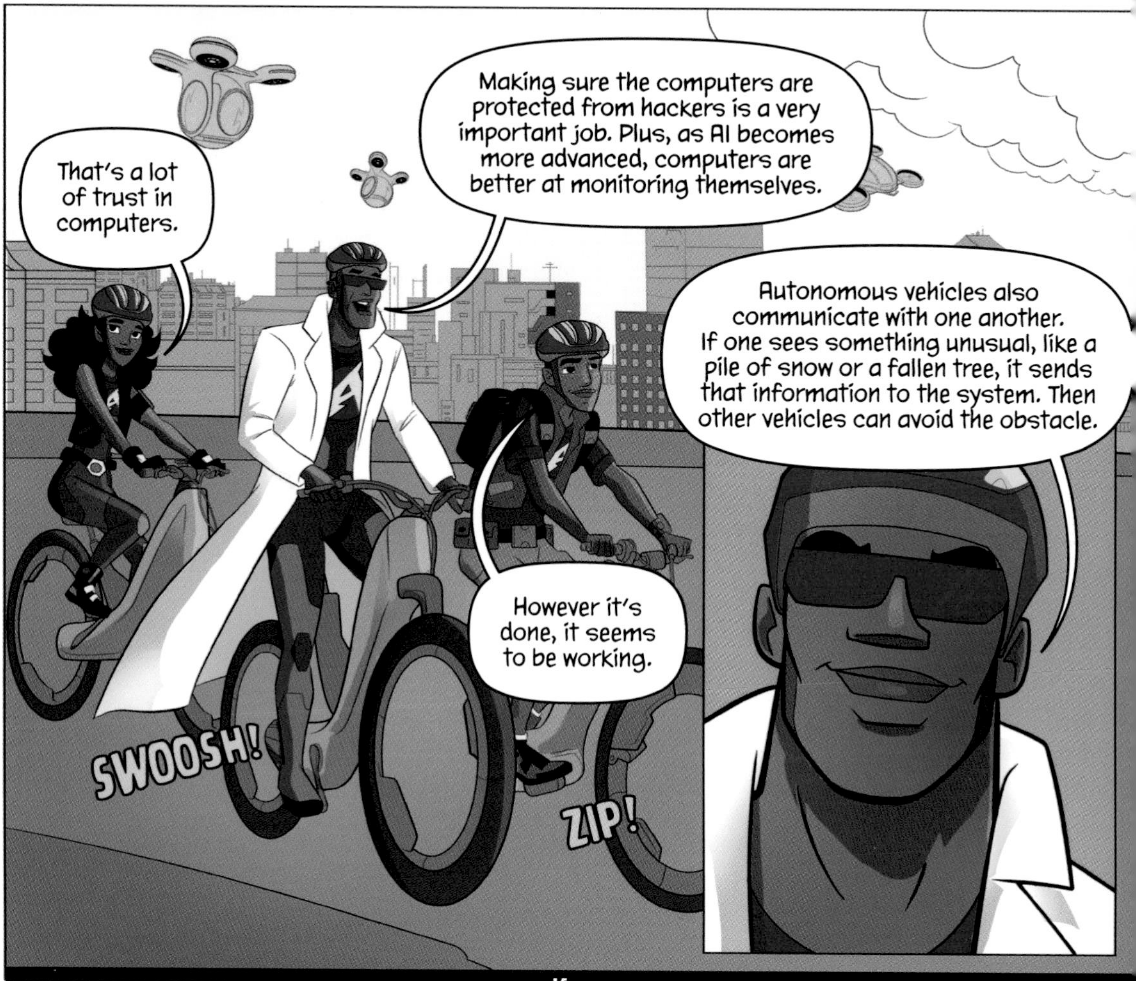
That's a lot of trust in computers.
Making sure the computers are protected from hackers is a very important job. Plus, as AI becomes more advanced, computers are better at monitoring themselves.
However it's done, it seems to be working.
Autonomous vehicles also communicate with one another. If one sees something unusual, like a pile of snow or a fallen tree, it sends that information to the system. Then other vehicles can avoid the obstacle.
SWOOSH!
ZIP!

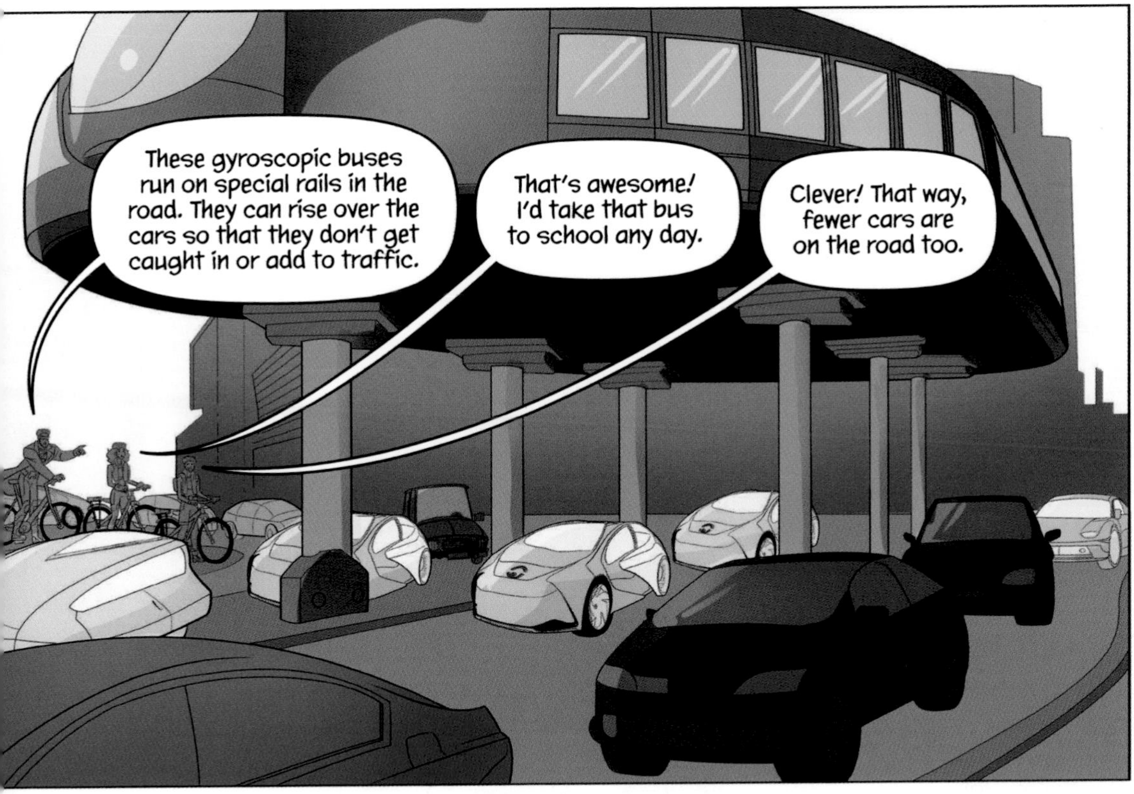
These gyroscopic buses run on special rails in the road. They can rise over the cars so that they don't get caught in or add to traffic.
That's awesome! I'd take that bus to school any day.
Clever! That way, fewer cars are on the road too.

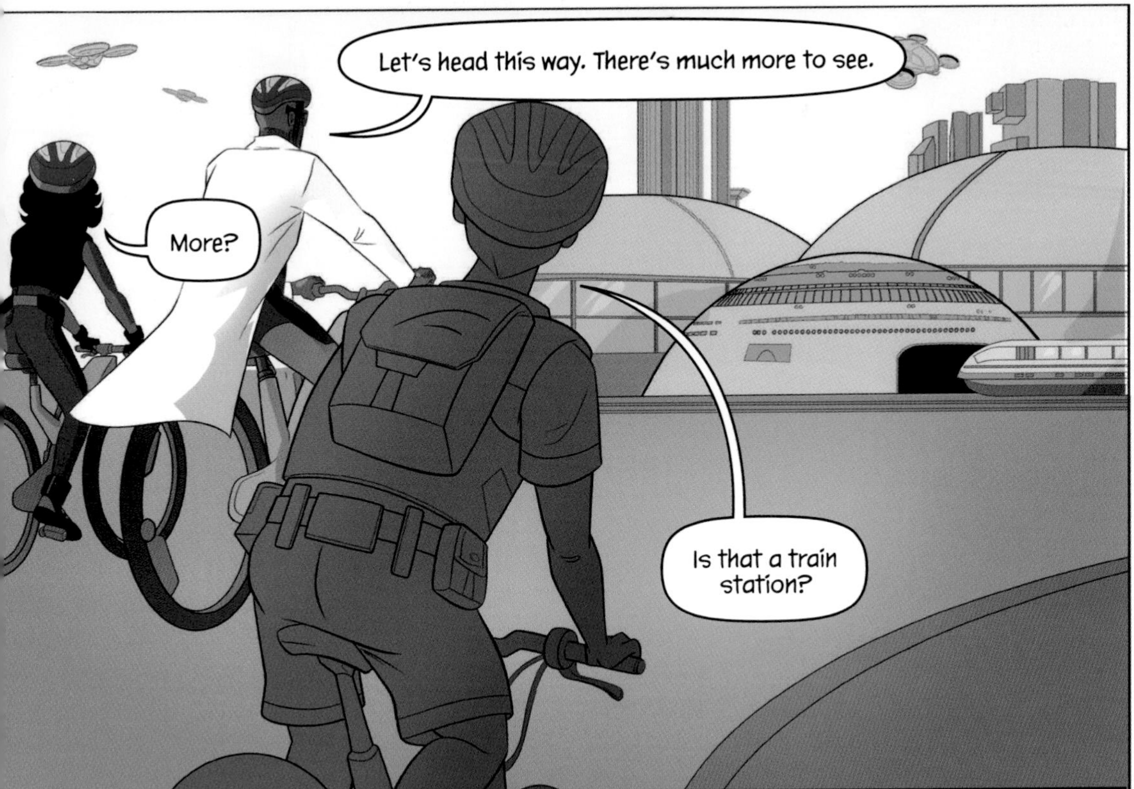
Let's head this way. There's much more to see.
More?
Is that a train station?

SECTION 3: LONG DISTANCE GROUND TRANSPORTATION

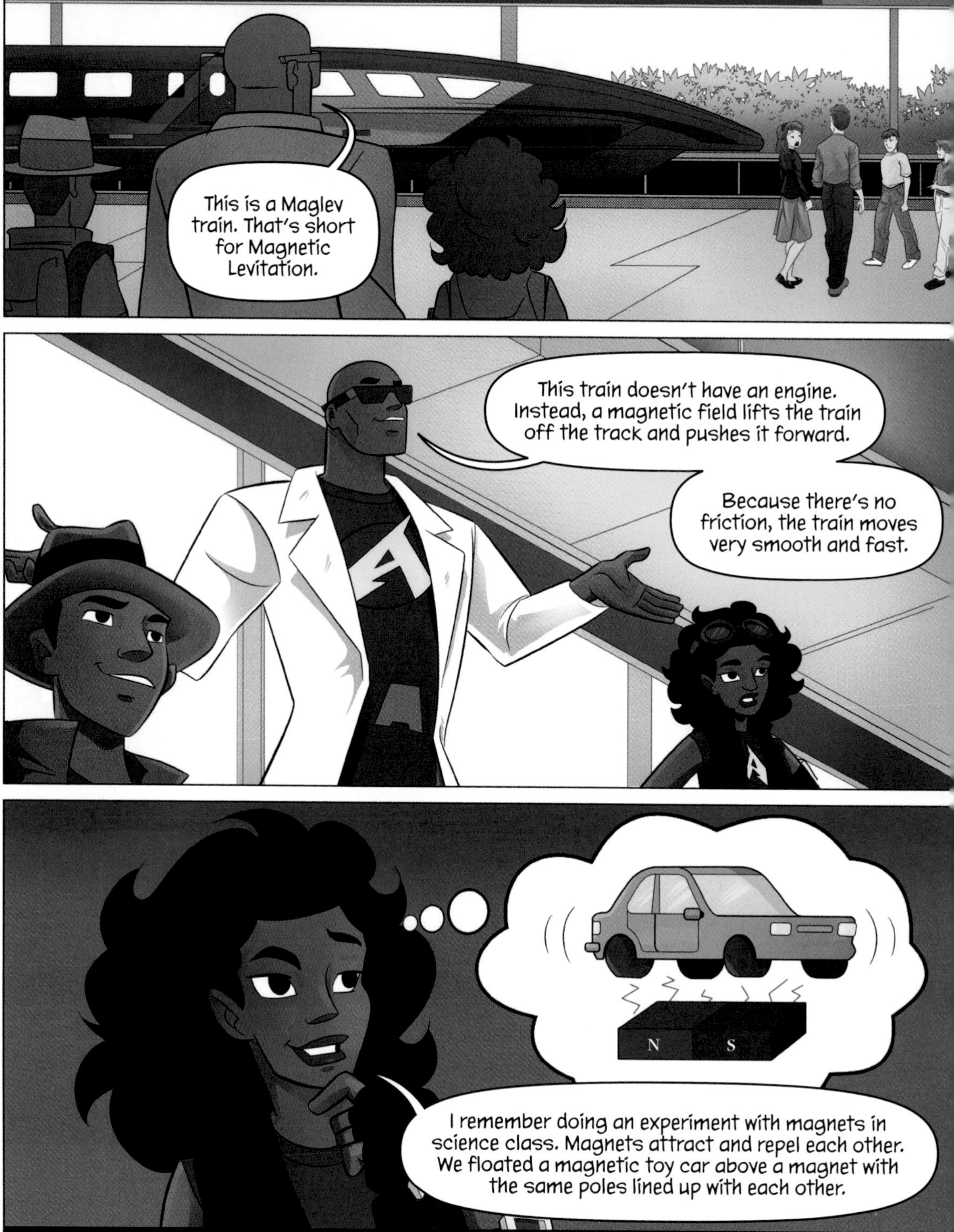

This is a Maglev train. That's short for Magnetic Levitation.
This train doesn't have an engine. Instead, a magnetic field lifts the train off the track and pushes it forward.
Because there's no friction, the train moves very smooth and fast.
N
S
I remember doing an experiment with magnets in science class. Magnets attract and repel each other. We floated a magnetic toy car above a magnet with the same poles lined up with each other.

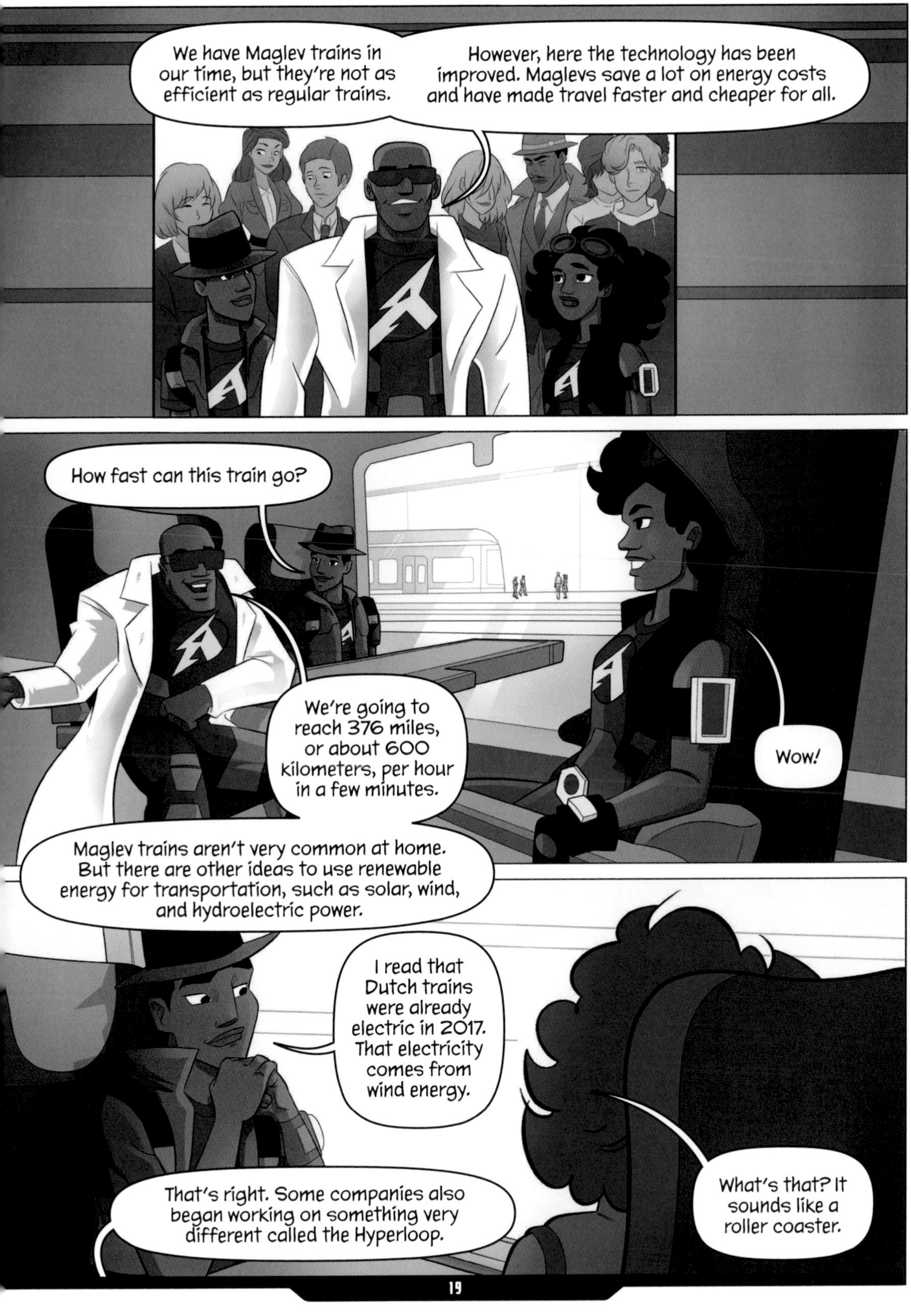
We have Maglev trains in our time, but they're not as efficient as regular trains.
However, here the technology has been improved. Maglevs save a lot on energy costs and have made travel faster and cheaper for all.
How fast can this train go?
We're going to reach 376 miles, or about 600 kilometers, per hour in a few minutes.
Wow!
Maglev trains aren't very common at home. But there are other ideas to use renewable energy for transportation, such as solar, wind, and hydroelectric power.
I read that Dutch trains were already electric in 2017. That electricity comes from wind energy.
That's right. Some companies also began working on something very different called the Hyperloop.
What's that? It sounds like a roller coaster.

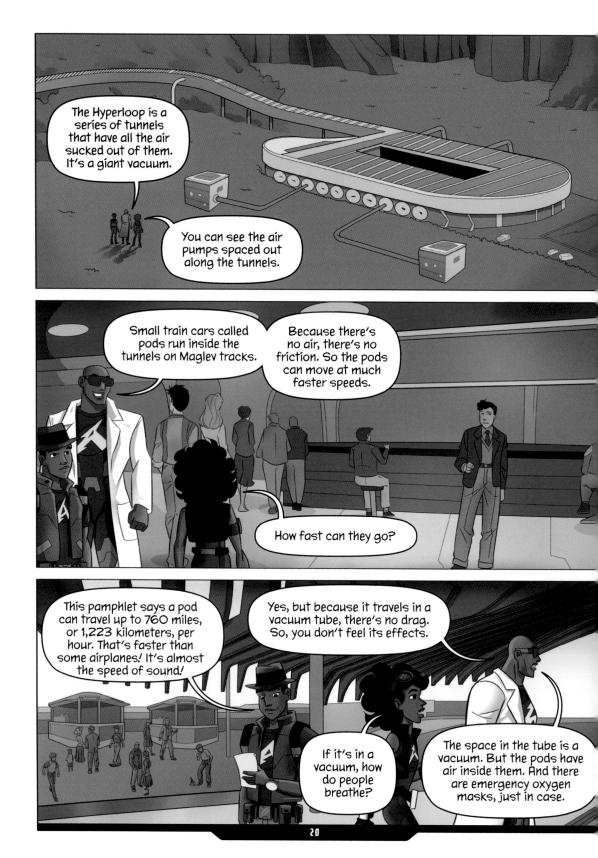

The Hyperloop is a series of tunnels that have all the air sucked out of them. It's a giant vacuum.

You can see the air pumps spaced out along the tunnels.

Small train cars called pods run inside the tunnels on Maglev tracks.

Because there's no air, there's no friction. So the pods can move at much faster speeds.

How fast can they go?

This pamphlet says a pod can travel up to 760 miles, or 1,223 kilometers, per hour. That's faster than some airplanes! It's almost the speed of sound!

Yes, but because it travels in a vacuum tube, there's no drag. So, you don't feel its effects.

If it's in a vacuum, how do people breathe?

The space in the tube is a vacuum. But the pods have air inside them. And there are emergency oxygen masks, just in case.

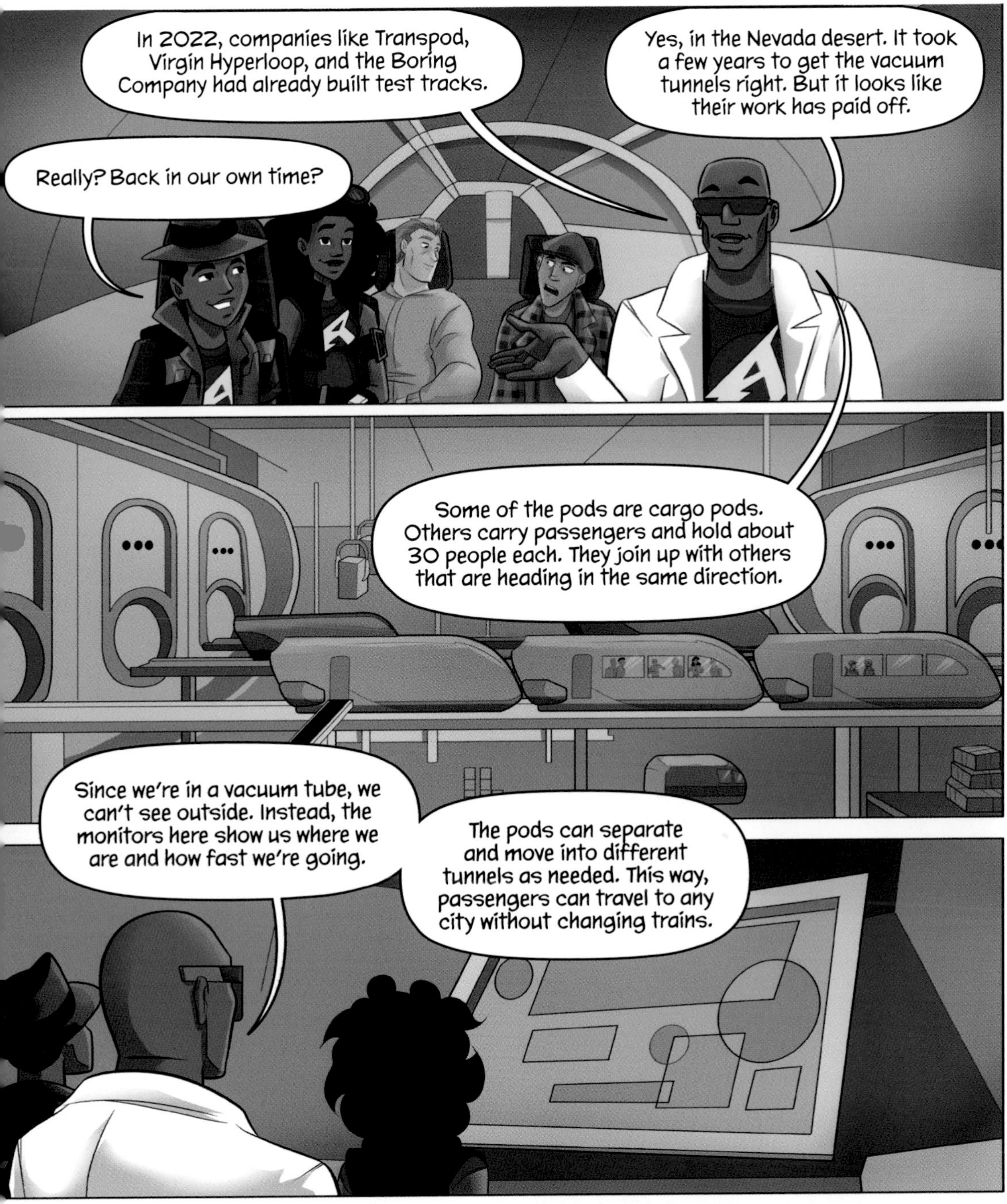
In 2022, companies like Transpod, Virgin Hyperloop, and the Boring Company had already built test tracks.
Yes, in the Nevada desert. It took a few years to get the vacuum tunnels right. But it looks like their work has paid off.
Really? Back in our own time?
Some of the pods are cargo pods. Others carry passengers and hold about 30 people each. They join up with others that are heading in the same direction.
Since we're in a vacuum tube, we can't see outside. Instead, the monitors here show us where we are and how fast we're going.
The pods can separate and move into different tunnels as needed. This way, passengers can travel to any city without changing trains.

RESISTING THE AIR

If you stick your hand out the window of a moving car, you can feel the wind push you back. This is air resistance, or friction. In a vacuum, there is no air to push back on an object. A vehicle inside a vacuum can travel very fast with no resistance.

SECTION 4: *THE FUTURE OF FLIGHT*

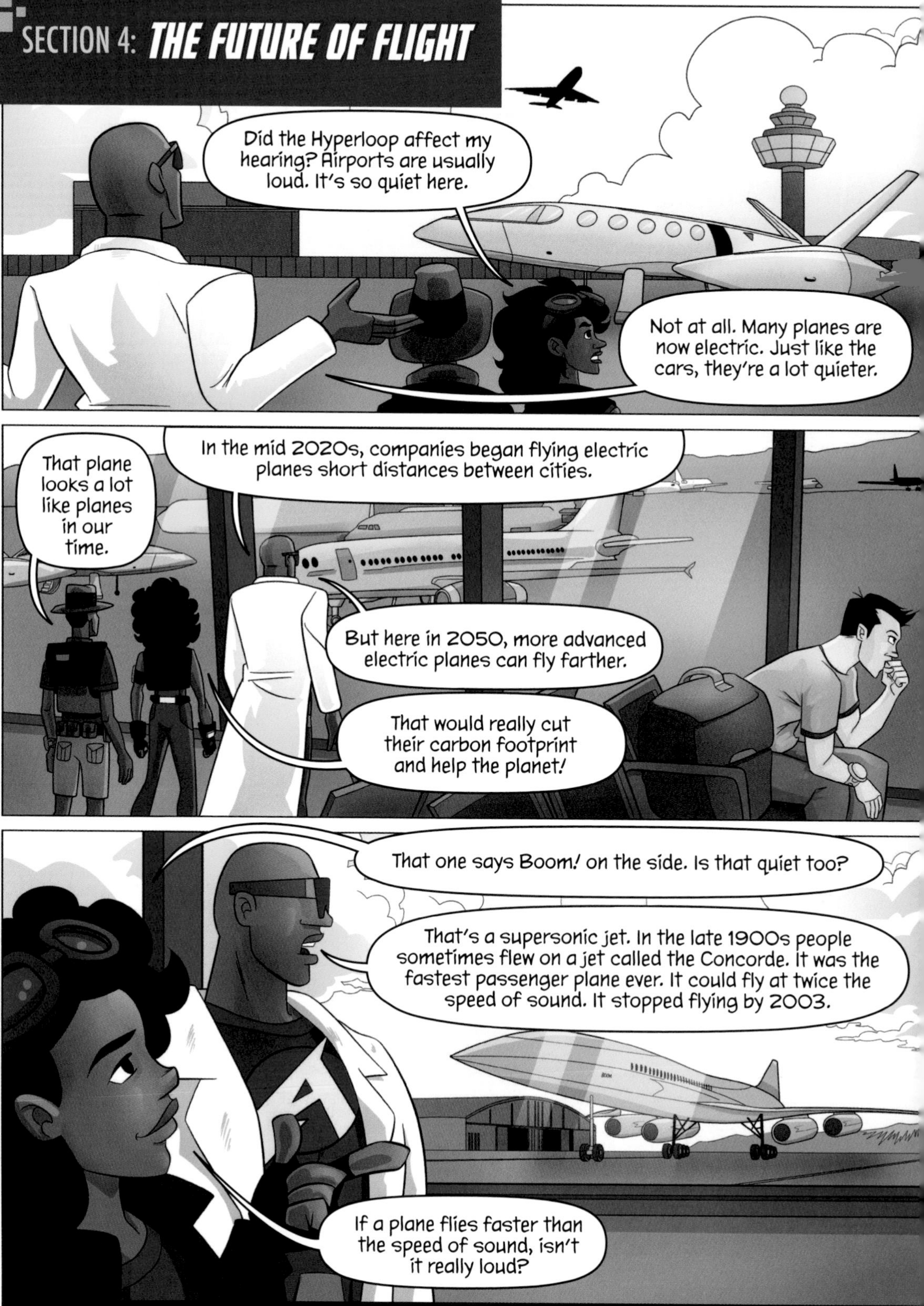

Did the Hyperloop affect my hearing? Airports are usually loud. It's so quiet here.
Not at all. Many planes are now electric. Just like the cars, they're a lot quieter.
That plane looks a lot like planes in our time.
In the mid 2020s, companies began flying electric planes short distances between cities.
But here in 2050, more advanced electric planes can fly farther.
That would really cut their carbon footprint and help the planet!
That one says Boom! on the side. Is that quiet too?
That's a supersonic jet. In the late 1900s people sometimes flew on a jet called the Concorde. It was the fastest passenger plane ever. It could fly at twice the speed of sound. It stopped flying by 2003.
If a plane flies faster than the speed of sound, isn't it really loud?

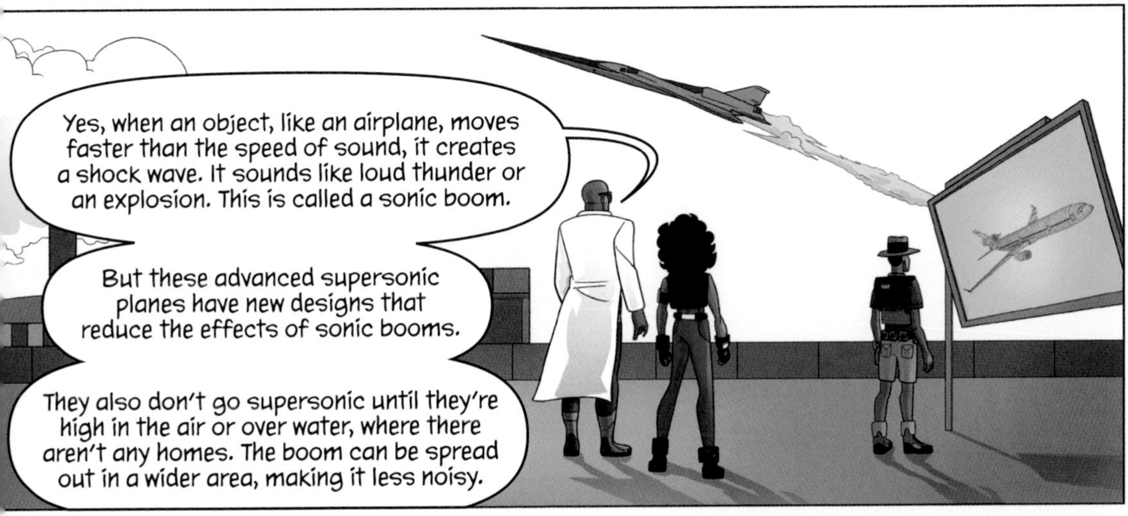
Yes, when an object, like an airplane, moves faster than the speed of sound, it creates a shock wave. It sounds like loud thunder or an explosion. This is called a sonic boom.
But these advanced supersonic planes have new designs that reduce the effects of sonic booms.
They also don't go supersonic until they're high in the air or over water, where there aren't any homes. The boom can be spread out in a wider area, making it less noisy.

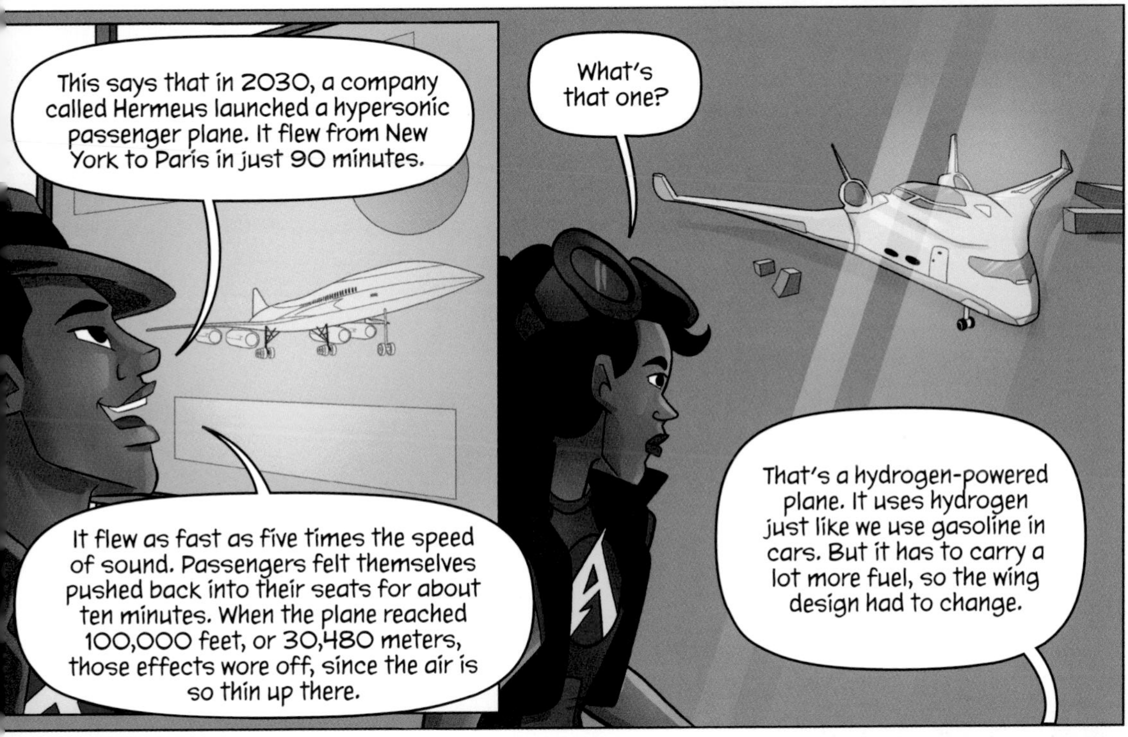
This says that in 2030, a company called Hermeus launched a hypersonic passenger plane. It flew from New York to Paris in just 90 minutes.
What's that one?
It flew as fast as five times the speed of sound. Passengers felt themselves pushed back into their seats for about ten minutes. When the plane reached 100,000 feet, or 30,480 meters, those effects wore off, since the air is so thin up there.
That's a hydrogen-powered plane. It uses hydrogen just like we use gasoline in cars. But it has to carry a lot more fuel, so the wing design had to change.

A HYDROGEN-FUELED PLANE?

Hydrogen can be cooled and stored in liquid form. Then it can be used to generate electricity that would power a plane. It could also be used like jet fuel to power the plane directly. There are still several dangers to overcome, but scientists are working to make the hydrogen plane a reality. If successful, it could help reduce the need for using fossil fuels.

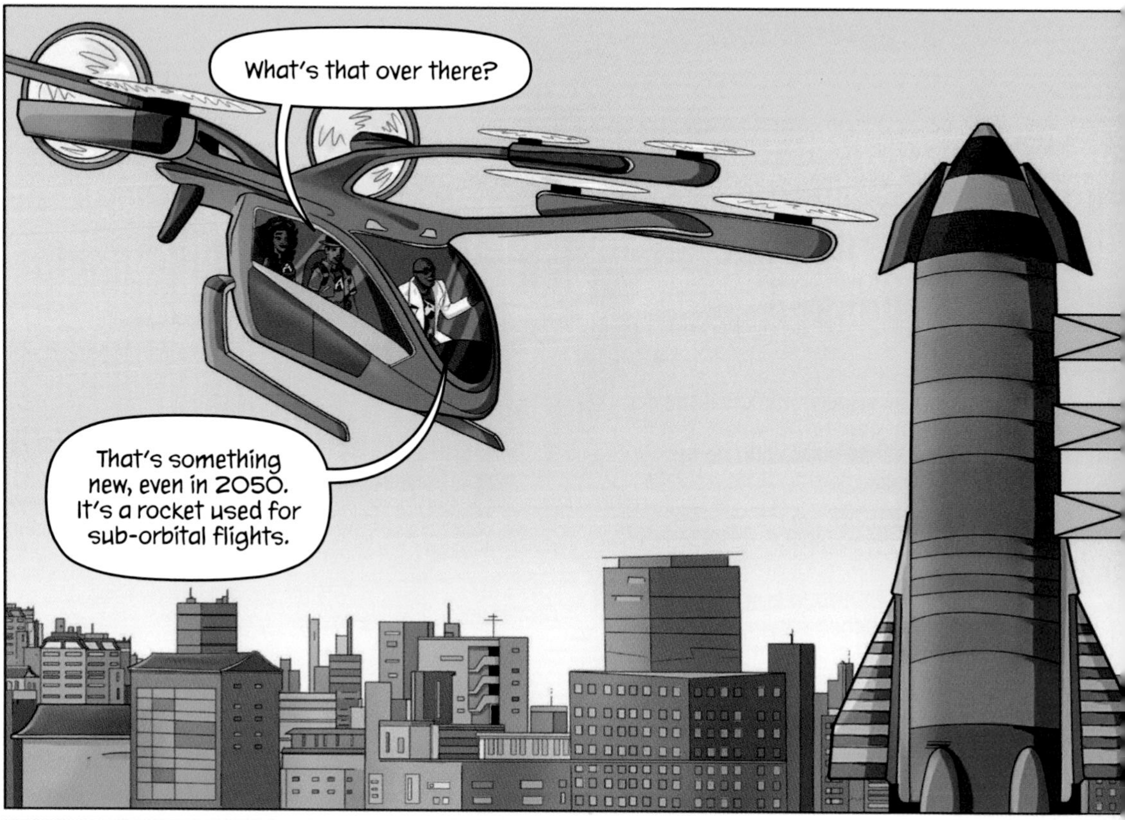
What's that over there?
That's something new, even in 2050. It's a rocket used for sub-orbital flights.

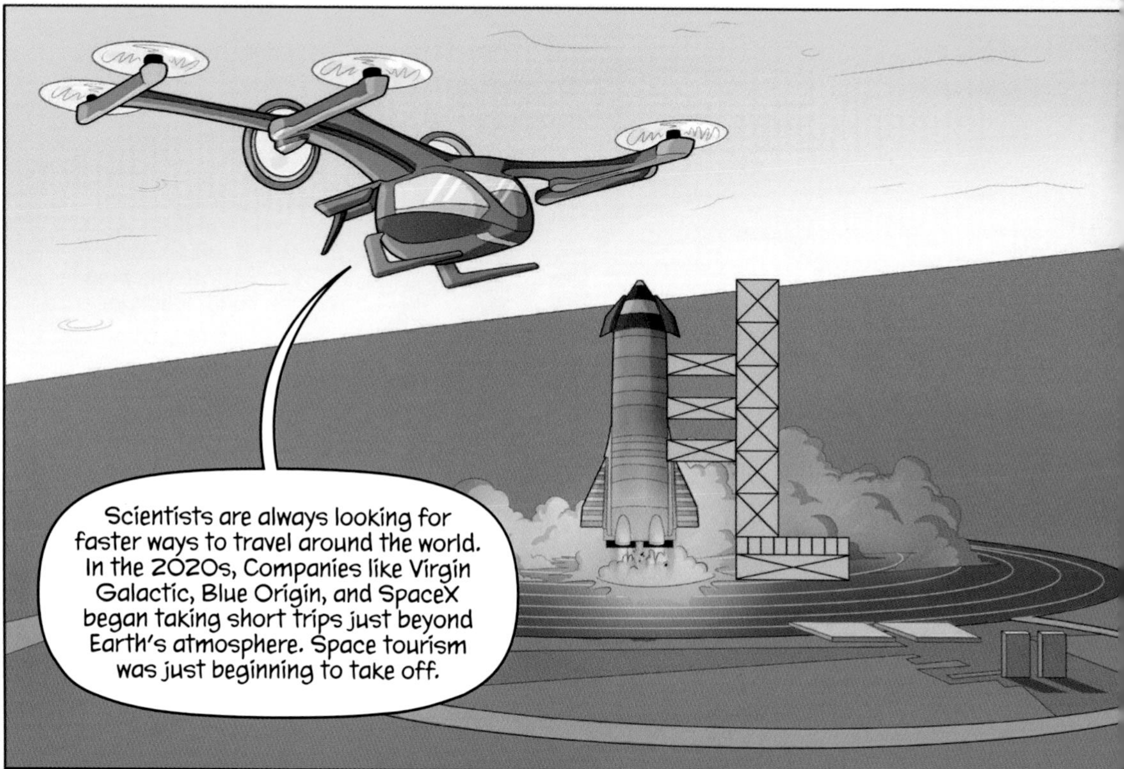
Scientists are always looking for faster ways to travel around the world. In the 2020s, Companies like Virgin Galactic, Blue Origin, and SpaceX began taking short trips just beyond Earth's atmosphere. Space tourism was just beginning to take off.

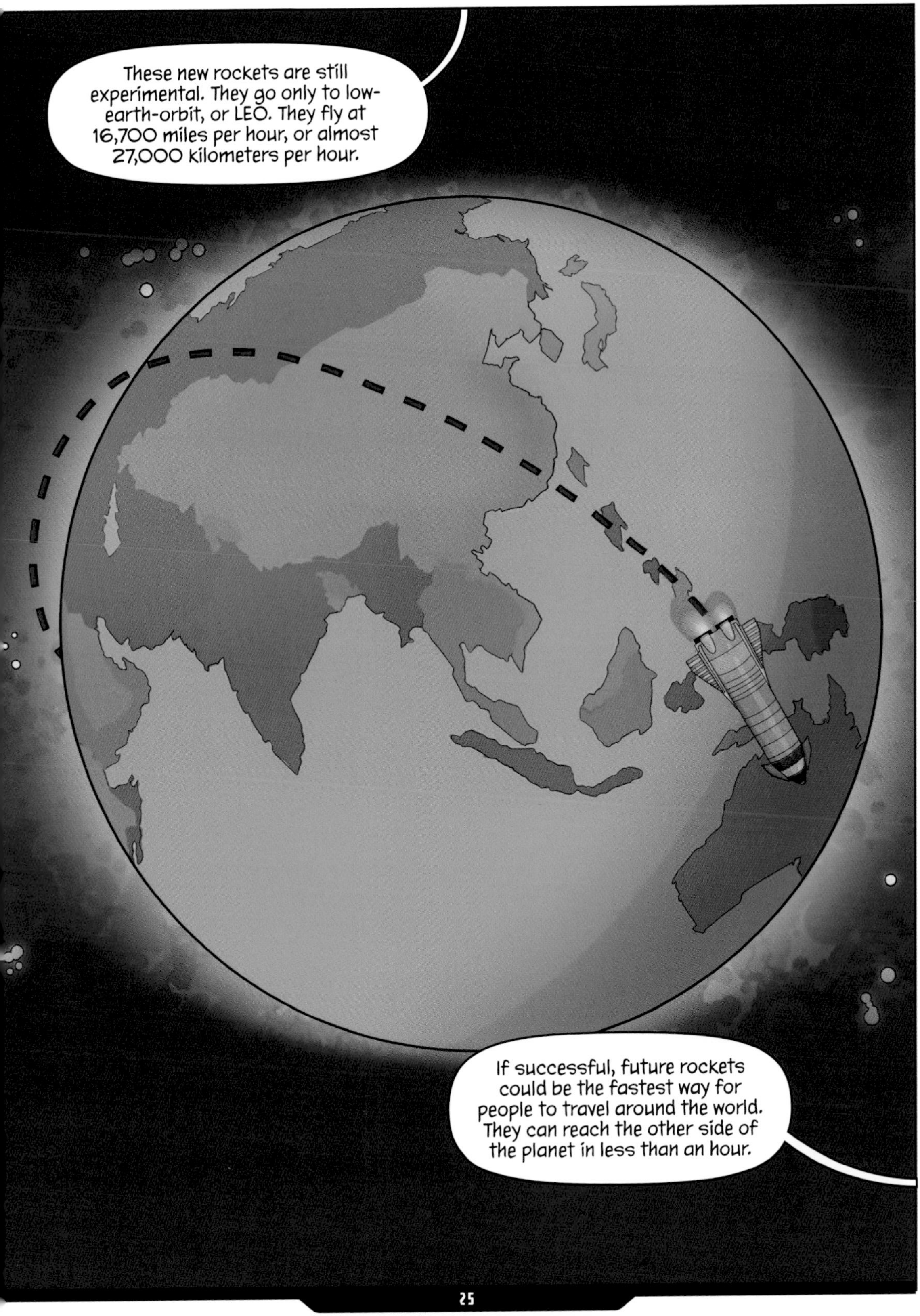
These new rockets are still experimental. They go only to low-earth-orbit, or LEO. They fly at 16,700 miles per hour, or almost 27,000 kilometers per hour.
If successful, future rockets could be the fastest way for people to travel around the world. They can reach the other side of the planet in less than an hour.

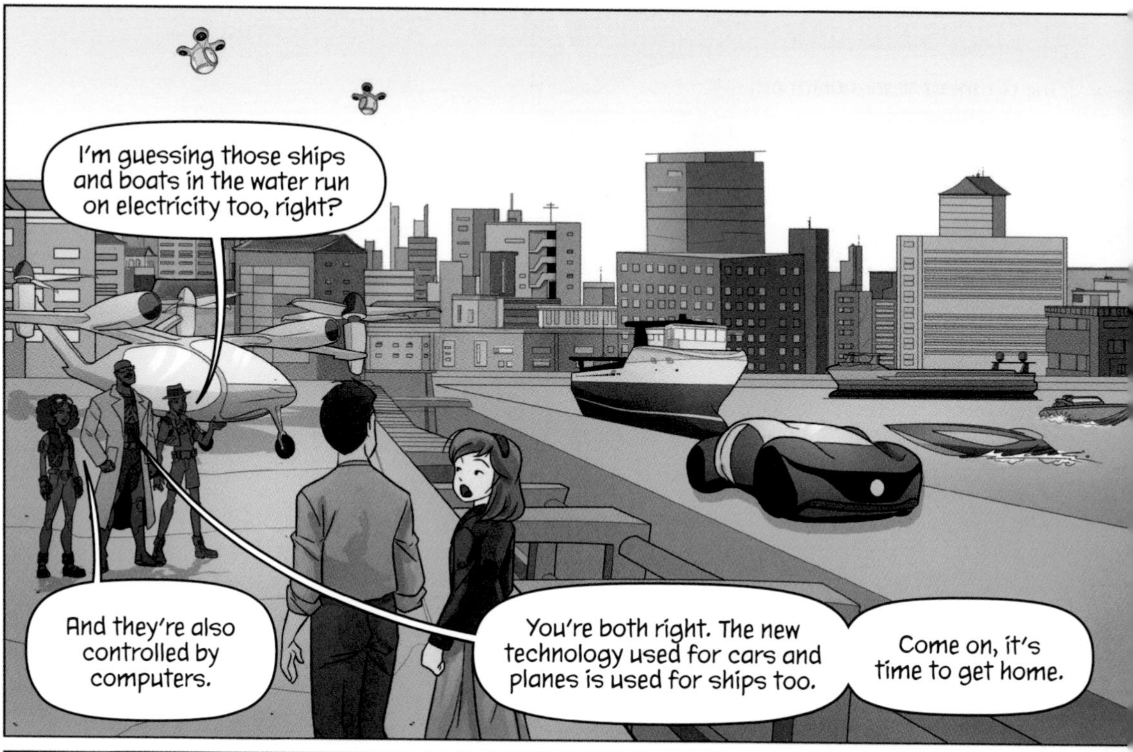
I'm guessing those ships and boats in the water run on electricity too, right?
And they're also controlled by computers.
You're both right. The new technology used for cars and planes is used for ships too.
Come on, it's time to get home.

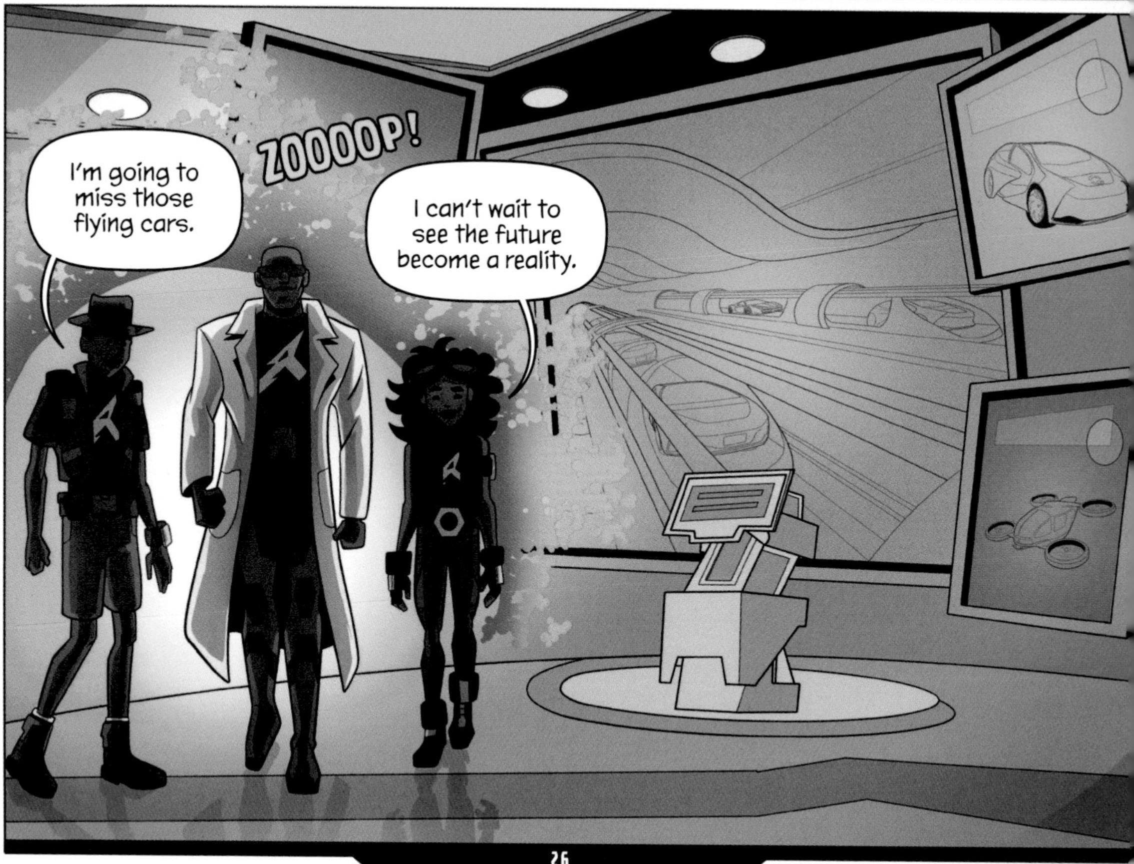
ZOOOOP!
I'm going to miss those flying cars.
I can't wait to see the future become a reality.

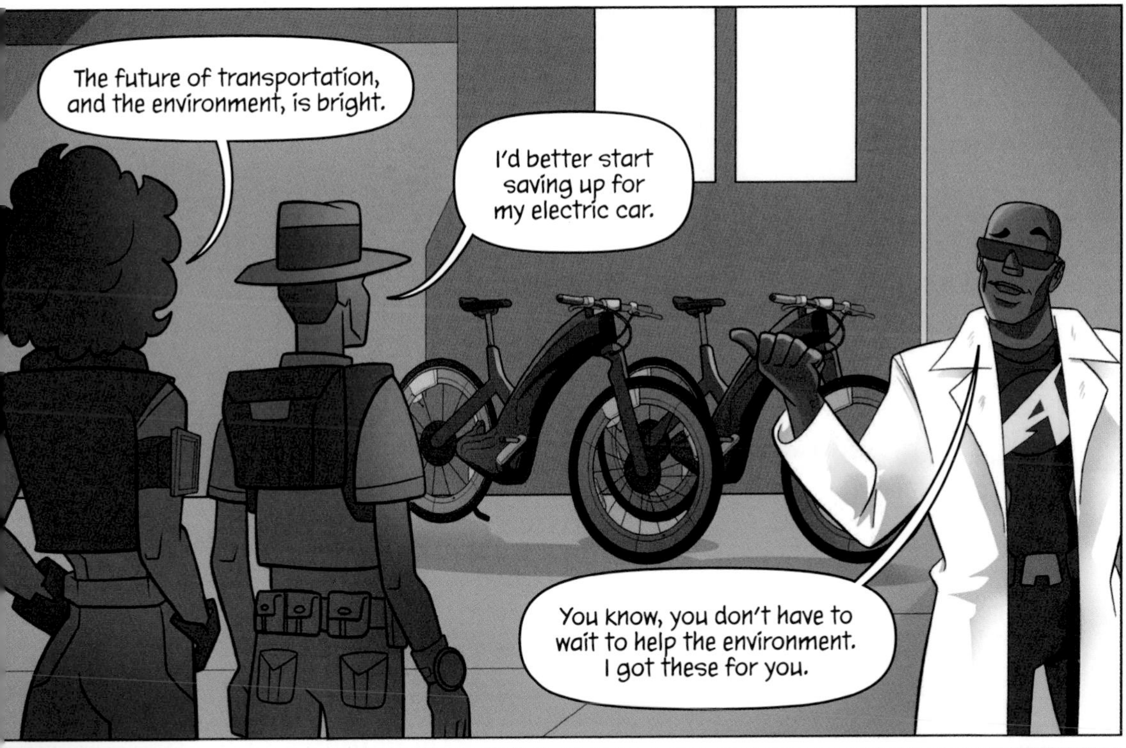
The future of transportation, and the environment, is bright.
I'd better start saving up for my electric car.
You know, you don't have to wait to help the environment. I got these for you.

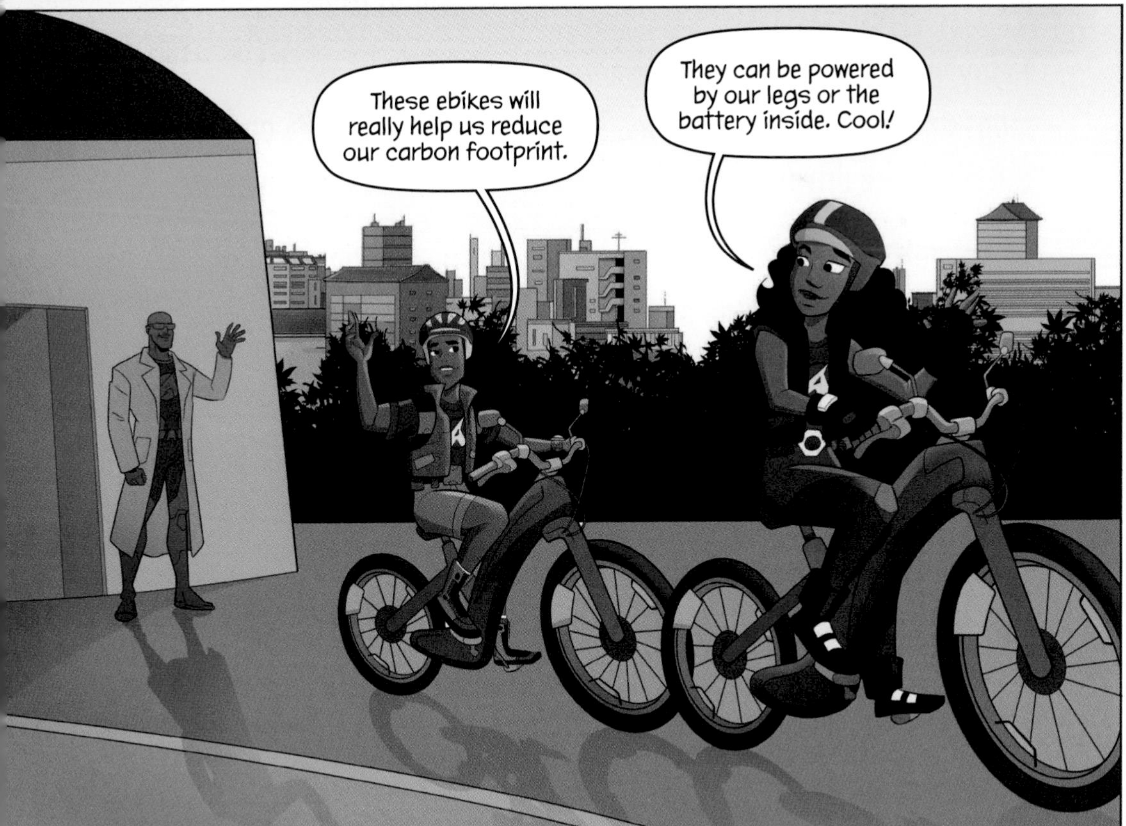
These ebikes will really help us reduce our carbon footprint.
They can be powered by our legs or the battery inside. Cool!

MORE ABOUT THE FUTURE OF TRANSPORTATION

Many new cars today have computers on board to help humans drive more safely. Some can sense objects around them and slow down or even stop when they get too close to another vehicle.

Some vehicles can suggest that the driver take a break during a long trip. Others also have a version of autopilot, where the driver only needs to keep a hand on the steering wheel. The car travels at the correct speed, at a safe distance from the car in front.

Today, many vehicles have computer systems that can provide maps and real-time traffic news. They are powered by GPS and can direct the driver to take the quickest route to their destination.

Completely autonomous cars, where there is no human driver at all, are still experimental. Some have been in accidents that forced companies to remove the self-driving cars from the road.

Countries like the United States, Japan, Germany, and South Korea are closer to having truly self-driving cars. They have better roads and greater support from their governments. But in the near future, self-driving cars may be a common sight on most roads.

Several companies have already begun using robotic delivery vehicles. Some travel along on sidewalks while others, such as delivery drones, fly overhead. Companies like Alibaba in China and Amazon.com in the United States are delivering packages to residents in cities without a human driver. These automated vehicles could soon become a regular sight in our neighborhoods. In some ways, the future of transportation has already arrived.

GLOSSARY

artificial intelligence (ar-tuh-FISH-uhl in-TEL-uh-juhnss)—the ability of a computer or machine to think and behave like a human

automated (AW-tuh-may-tuhd)—the use of machines to do work instead of people

autonomous (aw-TAH-nuh-muhss)—something, such as a vehicle or machine, that can control itself rather than be controlled by someone else

autopilot (AW-toh-py-luht)—a system on a vehicle that allows it to steer and control itself

carbon footprint (KAHR-buhn FOOT-print)—the amount of carbon dioxide released into the atmosphere by one's activities

drag (DRAG)—the force that resists the motion of an object moving through air

friction (FRIK-shuhn)—a force created when two objects rub together; friction slows down objects

GPS (GEE PEE ESS)—short for Global Positioning System; an electronic tool used to find the location of an object or directions to a certain location

gyroscopic (jahy-ruh-SKAH-pik)—the ability to turn freely in any direction while maintaining balance

hydroelectric (hye-droh-ih-LEK-trik)—making electric power from the force of moving water

radar (RAY-dahr)—a device that uses radio waves to track the location of objects

renewable energy (rih-NOO-uh-buhl EN-ur-jee)—power from sources that will not be used up, such as wind, water, and the Sun

READ MORE

Chandler, Matt. *The Tech Behind Self-Driving Cars*. North Mankato, MN: Capstone Press, 2020.

Kuromiya, Jun. *The Future of Transportation*. Minneapolis: Lerner Publications, 2021.

Klepeis, Alicia. *The Future of Transportation: From Electric Cars to Jet Packs*. North Mankato, MN: Capstone Press, 2020.

INTERNET SITES

Alternative Fuel Vehicle Facts
kids.kiddle.co/Alternative_fuel_vehicle

Energy Kids
eia.gov/kids/

Future Transportation
thezebra.com/resources/driving/future-transportation/#infographic

ABOUT THE AUTHOR

Ailynn Collins has written several nonfiction children's books about amazing people, space, and science. Ailynn also loves to write fiction, especially stories about aliens, ghosts, witches, dinosaurs, and traveling through the universe. She lives outside Seattle, Washington, with her husband and five dogs.

ABOUT THE ILLUSTRATOR

Daniel Pedrosa was born in Araraquara, a quiet town in São Paulo, Brazil. Since he was a child he has always had an interest in art. At the age of ten, his older brother gave him his first superhero comic. It was then he decided that drawing comics would be his profession. In 2010, he began his professional career doing comic strips for newspapers and drawing children's supplements for tabloids and magazines. Today Daniel creates colorful art for Criptozoik, Tildawave, Capstone, 137 Studios, and produces advertising material for the largest Honda Motors store in Brazil.